6.00/1

D0501822

Public Diplomacy and

the Behavioral Sciences

Public Diplomacy and

the Behavioral Sciences

GLEN H. FISHER

 Indiana University Press

BLOOMINGTON / LONDON

Copyright © 1972 by Indiana University Press
All rights reserved

No part of this book may be reproduced or utilized in any form
or by any means, electronic or mechanical, including photocopying
and recording, or by any information storage and retrieval system,
without permission in writing from the publisher. The Association
of American University Presses' Resolution on Permissions constitutes
the only exception to this prohibition.

Published in Canada by Fitzhenry & Whiteside Limited,
Don Mills, Ontario
Library of Congress catalog card number: 76-180490
ISBN: 0-253-34670-3 LL   0-253-34671-1 PA
Manufactured in the United States of America

UNIVERSITY LIBRARY
Lethbridge, Alberta
11763

Contents

Preface

As we confront each new international rela-
tions problem, we hope that it can be resolved by negotiation
and the art of diplomacy. Yet no one seems to be very sure just
what this "art" is. As the subject matter of international relations
continues to become more complicated, methods are being developed to cope with some of the technical and repetitive issues
in more rational and orderly ways. International terminology,
objective criteria, and legal standards have evolved to enhance
communication and understanding in such fields as economic
and monetary relations, trade and transportation agreements,
and military alliances. Still, resolution of many issues depends
on surmounting that elusive human element which brings negotiation and diplomacy back to intuitive and subjective skills.
International communication is complicated as it passes cultural
boundaries. It is never easy to comprehend motivation and
psychological reaction.

In a search for more rational and objective ways to probe the
human element in foreign affairs, we would expect that the behavioral sciences, almost by definition, should be the source
of new and scientifically oriented insight into why people,

singly and in groups, do what they do and think what they think. As the main disciplines involved have matured—especially psychology, sociology, and anthropology—the logical question has been why, if social scientists are reasonably competent, are we no further ahead in mastering the most pressing human problem of all, the international behavior of nations. Does behavioral science have a contribution to make to foreign affairs?

A few professional behavioral scientists have sought ways to extend their skills in this direction, with good effect. But they have found it difficult to gear into the problems of foreign affairs in such a way that those most involved in managing the complicated machinery of international relations can take their counsel into account. On the other hand, people with a primary interest in foreign affairs, and especially the professionals, have felt a need to reach out for more reliable ways of coping with the cultural and psychological dimension of their field of responsibility. They have seen science solve an amazing array of problems in diverse fields from medicine to warfare. They are aware of living in a computerized and automated world. Hence they look for similar breakthroughs in the behavioral sciences, albeit with some suspicion that one cannot be scientific about human behavior, and with a lingering confusion regarding the term "behavioral," which sounds too much like the outmoded deterministic "behaviorism" of a few decades ago. Further, their experience in using behavioral scientists has not been altogether satisfactory; they have not known how to choose and use them to best advantage, and academic men understandably have often required too much time to grasp the questions in unfamiliar, fast-moving operations. The fact that political scientists, and particularly those studying comparative politics, have incorporated considerable portions of the behavioral approach into their theory and methodology has improved matters. Still, the result is something of a standoff.

What, then, is the most practical way to tap some of the potential benefits of applied behavioral science? Should more behavioral scientists be employed? Should more money be spent on research projects? Should more foreign affairs specialists be sent back to the universities for behavioral science training? My present judgment is that an important first step requires that the people seriously concerned with foreign affairs activities become somewhat more proficient themselves in using basic behavioral science approaches and some of the conceptual tools available, as part of their professional competence. In international relations problems at the present stage of development, the genius of behavioral scientists is not necessarily found in the answers they have produced or in the sophistication of their research methodology. It is in their more effective way of looking at problems which have a psychological or cross-cultural component, their way of using concepts to provide order and meaning to observations, and often, their way of simply asking the right questions. Ordinarily the foreign affairs specialist will not have a trained research team at his side or a computer to process data. His analysis and interpretation of his "data" will go on in his own mind, whether this situation is the ideal one or not. Therefore, capturing a behavioral-science point of view and conceptual approach may be the first objective.

Unfortunately the several academic disciplines involved along with their considerably proliferated subfields have generated a forbidding jungle of definitions, jargon, paradigms, models, and methodological constructs. This is all the more true as the labor-saving computer invites manipulation of data in many new ways and toward more diverse theoretical purposes. This state of affairs is not only disconcerting to the nonspecialist but also tends to place the behavioral science field outside the reasonable limits of personal intervention. If the foreign affairs specialist is to use these resources at all, he needs a digestible selection of the more fundamental, widely used, and proven conceptual components.

In the public diplomacy context expanding international communication is coming to be an increasingly important factor in the actual outcome of foreign policy decisions and overseas programs. The urgency of this reality plus the circumstance that, as a Foreign Service officer with a behavioral science background, I already have a foot in each side of this problem, prompts me to set forth my proposal for a combination of cultural and psychological approaches. My discussion is directed toward my colleagues in the foreign affairs community, and beyond them to students and to the public interested in the psychological and cultural dimension of foreign affairs. I have chosen perception and its relationship to culture as a starting point, and as a central thread to which additional concepts can be systematically related. This has the advantage of starting with a concept generally familiar to the reader, and, I hope, making subsequent, less familiar ideas appear more logical. The behavioral scientist will find little in this book that is new, but it may indicate to him the areas in which behavioral science can contribute the most. For the foreign affairs professional, this book offers a medium range of behavioral science orientation.

Perhaps the unusual combination of a behavioral science background and an assortment of regular Foreign Service assignments has given me a unique vantage point for approaching this subject. From time to time I have tried to put this experience to use. I have been assigned three times to the State Department's Foreign Service Institute, an in-service training institution for U.S. government personnel who work overseas. The first time I served as a resource specialist in the behavioral sciences; the second time this role was combined with responsibility for coordinating a series of area study programs; and now I am in charge of the Center for Area and Country Studies. At various stages my attention has ranged from problems of individual adaptation to working in a foreign culture, through techniques for understanding the structure and function of foreign institutions, to looking for the effects which cultural and psychological aspects of the international communication process have on the outcome of policies and overseas programs.

In the course of my foreign service duties I have frequently considered working this material into a book, but occasion, time, and access to academic facilities were never sufficient. For providing these, I am deeply grateful to the Department of State for arranging a break in assignments to undertake this project, and to the faculty of the Fletcher School of Law and Diplomacy at Tufts University for allowing me to join them and enjoy the intellectual stimulation of their professional company while pursuing my special interest. The newly-created Edward R. Murrow Center of Public Diplomacy, a part of the Fletcher School, has been a particularly congenial home base for my pursuit.

Views and opinions expressed here are, of course, mine, and do not necessarily reflect those of the United States government or the Department of State.

G.H.F.

July 1971

Public Diplomacy and

the Behavioral Sciences

I

The Relevance of

the Behavioral Sciences to

Modern Diplomacy

IT IS OBVIOUS FROM DAY-TO-DAY EXPERIENCE IN the various foreign affairs establishments around the world that diplomacy is simply not what it used to be. Expanding communications technology and a greater public participation in the foreign affairs process make much of the difference. The change was signaled at the end of World War I, when President Wilson called for open covenants, openly arrived at. And changes were well advanced by the end of World War II, when the publics of several countries wanted to know what happened at Yalta and related conferences, questioning both the decisions and the propriety even in wartime of such far-reaching decisions being made without the voice of the people most directly concerned. The public's deference to their leaders' wisdom in international relations has diminished markedly in recent years. "Secret diplomacy" has become almost a contradiction of terms.

Today's diplomats still read the late Sir Harold Nicolson's 1939 classic, *Diplomacy*, but with more of a nostalgic concern for their image than as a realistic guide to diplomatic practice.[1]

While much of Nicolson's treatment of the negotiation process and of the personal qualities necessary to practice the diplomatic art is still relevant, today's professional works with the realization that a great deal more goes into the relationships between nations than the skillfulness of individual negotiators. At the very least, the decision maker and the negotiator find their range of alternatives constrained by the mood and viewpoint of their interested publics. They must work as hard to find the points of agreement which will sell at home as to find those points which will be acceptable abroad. And what will be accepted abroad depends on meeting not only the mind of the other government's representative but that of his interested public as well.

Actually Nicolson was aware of the trend thirty years ago. He called it "democratic diplomacy." While recognizing the virtues of greater public participation in international affairs, he foresaw complications in pursuing the comfortable and traditional diplomatic style described in his writings. He did not seem pleased with the prospect.

The great increase in information which flows across national boundaries in the public news media, whether accurate or not, changes the reporting function of embassies. Embassy reports and analyses now compete as never before with those of reporters, travelers, and other officials which may reach the home public and government officials first. Thus the diplomat's judgment, professional and reasoned though it may be, is immediately diluted by the points of view of other reporters and by the reaction of interested domestic observers. Further, embassy officials abroad find increasingly that they must become adept in communicating not only with the officials of the government to which they are accredited but also beyond them with the foreign public. It is not enough to be sure that their counterparts in the foreign office understand their country's policy; the people whose opinions and attitudes will come to bear on that foreign office must understand it too.

Thus we see that it is the explosion in participation in international affairs accompanying the revolution in communication that makes diplomacy of the 1970s so different. The way a large public perceives an issue at hand, reasons about it, and responds to it becomes an integral factor in international relations, and therefore in policy formation and execution.[2]

Another way of describing the changing times in diplomacy is to say that today's reality in foreign affairs is found less in the formal dimension of international relations and more in the informal and even "irrational" dimension which involves the knowledge, prejudices, attitudes, and opinions of participating masses of people. That is to say, it is less exclusively a matter of conference-table negotiations, where diplomats can put emotion aside, refer to their position papers, and deal with diplomatic counterparts who share a certain established system of logic regarding international issues and the way to negotiate them. In less complicated days the objective argument, the precisely written message, the appeal to precedence and international law counted for more. Everyone involved had a fairly clear view of the facts and the range of obtainable objectives. Thus Sir Harold Nicolson could write a manual for Western professionals which the newcomer of his day would be well-advised to review. But in 1967 the widespread belief in Egypt that the United States had encouraged and even participated in the Israeli action against Egypt in the Six-Day War was a "fact" which a clarification at the foreign office could not alter.

Today's reality thus calls for some proficiency in dealing with the less formal and less rational, with international communication, and with the processes by which public perception and opinion are translated into governmental responses. Understandably, foreign affairs establishments, like other institutions, prefer not to change their basic assumptions, their structure, or their ways of doing things. Even so, they have been adapting to these new circumstances. Diplomatic lists for embassies of many countries now include press attachés, cultural affairs officers, information officers, labor attachés, etc., all of whom are relatively new in the structure of diplomatic missions. The United States Information Service is one of the most prominent examples of fortifying communications capabilities abroad, but it is by no means alone. The efforts of other nations range from similar agencies down to paid lobbyists, as well as to a wide variety of government-sponsored efforts by official press and radio to reach the public in other countries.[3]

As the public psychological dimension has reached the importance that it now has in both bilateral and multilateral international relations, those most directly and professionally involved have been faced with a task of becoming more technically competent in the psychology of international communication. We say "more" technically competent because most foreign affairs specialists start with considerable proficiency. They possess experience, greater or less insight into the nature of foreign civilizations and cultures, and a politician's sense of issues. But such competence tends to be individualized, often intuitive. It is more art than science when dealing with the emotional and attitudinal factors which so often appear irrational in their cross-cultural conflict of meaning, and which, while popular in scope, tend to be diffuse and intangible in assessment. At the least, better conceptual and intellectual tools are needed to make the analysis of these factors clearer and more objective.

Even after we accept the fact that this fundamental change in the nature of international relations has taken place, it is not enough simply to apply greater competence in the psychology of foreign affairs to expedite a policy or to make it more palatable. The skill must be used in choosing international actions in the first place which can be expected to gain the desired objectives *because* consideration has been given to the probable perception and response factors to which they will be subjected. This consideration is highly important. It means a willingness to come to grips with the psychological dimension of foreign affairs at the policy deliberation stage, not merely at the public relations stage after the fact.

The contribution which our space exploration program has made to American stature in the international arena was clearly increased by our decision to let the world share in the adventure with full publicity, extensive explanation of the missions, and an acknowledgement that the genius which culminated in successful space technology was multinational.

On the other hand, news analysts who followed Governor Rockefeller's 1969 fact-finding trip to Latin America pointed out that the canceled invitations and turbulent receptions which reduced the trip's accomplishment could have been forecast. They noted that the plan for the trip did not anticipate the intensity of the feeling which associates anxieties about "imperialism" with stereotyped images of the Rockefeller family name and the petroleum company associated with it, and that this factor would so strongly affect perceptions of his trip.

Currently we are making a significant step forward in coping with the psychological aspect of international relations by legitimizing and naming this new offspring in the family of international relations studies. We now speak of "public diplomacy" as a field of specialized professional interest and as an academic subdiscipline. For example, in 1965 the Fletcher School of Law and Diplomacy, a graduate school in international relations with a long-standing reputation for training students for careers in international affairs, established the Edward R. Murrow Center of Public Diplomacy. The Center sees public diplomacy as encompassing "the cause and effect of public attitudes and opinions which influence the formulation and execution of foreign policies," and proposes to treat a dimension of international relations beyond traditional diplomacy. It is a center for study and research in international communication, broadly defined, and for a practical study program for those who wish to concentrate in this field or use it to supplement major interests in other aspects of international relations. The decision to add the Center to this rather specialized graduate school stems from specific recognition of the growing importance of public diplomacy.[4]

Other indicators which establish the new field include a

report by a subcommittee of the House Foreign Affairs Committee, "The Future of United States Public Diplomacy," [5] which is somewhat narrowly directed toward the U.S. "image" as a factor in U.S. diplomacy. But it speaks of an "age of public diplomacy." In 1969 the Senate Committee on Foreign Relations held hearings on "Psychological Aspects of Foreign Policy." [6] The Peace Corps certainly was conceived with an age of public diplomacy in mind.

Thus, modern diplomats, policy makers, and scholars in international affairs are coming to realize that the actual consequences of a given policy initiative or overseas program are determined not only by that policy's logic as understood in government-to-government relations, or by the skill used in presenting and executing the policy in traditional diplomatic ways, but also by how both the domestic and the foreign publics perceive the issues and the policy offered. This understanding depends partly, of course, on the way in which the communications media—formal and informal—present the picture. But it depends more profoundly on the complex of knowledge, attitudes, and prejudices we have stressed above.

The Alliance for Progress in Latin America is a case in point. Despite the careful wording in Punta del Este in 1961, which established that the Alliance was a *mutual* agreement of the countries involved to work together, invest together, and seek resources together, and despite the agreement on the part of the participating countries to take deliberate action to achieve internal social, economic, and administrative reforms, most of Latin America *perceived* the alliance as a unilateral U.S. program which promised more U.S. funds for a ten-year period of revolutionary development. Latin Americans up to the level of cabinet minister shared this misperception and responded to Alliance projects accordingly. The consequences of the Alliance for Progress can be understood only by taking into account this dimension of misperception and inappropriate response along with other more apparent factors.

Dealing with psychological factors is exceptionally frustrating. By their nature they seem to be unreasoned, unpredictable, inscrutable, and emotionally laden. It is difficult enough to work with these factors after a policy is launched; to take them into account while policies are being chosen and programs are being devised is even harder, with the problem of predictability further confounding the task. Yet this is precisely what intelligent public diplomacy asks if the response on the part of the other government and its public is to come closer to that contemplated in the making of a policy decision. We have only to recall the miscalculation of Cuban public response at the time of the Bay of Pigs initiative to dramatize the importance of accurately understanding the psychological dimension.

In theory, a need to increase competence in public diplomacy has been accepted. The trouble is that at the present stage of the development of public diplomacy psychological factors are dealt with mostly in a hit-or-miss, trial-and-error way. Some use is being made of public-opinion surveys, along with related research. Often such studies address themselves to rather vague information such as the status of U.S. prestige. Further studies have been contracted for by government agencies. Results have been uneven. The considerable controversy which followed the so-called Camelot project in Chile (never actually formally proposed or undertaken), in which various sociopsychological factors were to be surveyed in relation to political development, has left social scientists feeling compromised, and hence less cooperative. Most often the policy maker, individually or in committee, simply projects his own assumptions in judging psychological reactions to a given course of action, or in anticipating how issues will be handled by the communications media. At best the cumulative experience of area specialists within the foreign affairs establishment will be used.

Realistically we cannot expect much satisfaction from such an amateur approach. A fully developed public diplomacy will require much more precise conceptual and observational tools, approaches, and methods of analysis. As a new dimension of international relations, public diplomacy will involve nontraditional fields of inquiry. With international and intercultural communication the new center of attention, we must now emphasize the disciplines which study values, idea patterns, and world view in different social structures. In short, we are dealing with the subjects which usually fall within the interests of the behavioral sciences, especially social psychology, cultural anthropology, and sociology. While none of these fields normally have considered international relations to be their preserve, and they have only occasionally interested themselves in international communication, they have developed more efficient ways of handling the general subjects involved. We should not have to develop a new and separate psychological science just for public diplomacy, at least not until we have taken full advantage of those already developed which can be adapted to the needs of the foreign affairs specialist.

The premise of this book is that the behavioral sciences do hold scientifically developed concepts, knowledge, analytical procedures, and data which have been well-matured and tested. We recognize that large parts of these disciplines are not directly applicable, and some prejudice against their use in foreign affairs has been generated when they have been improperly used. However, with proper selection and adaptation, these disciplines suggest an intellectual orientation which could contribute considerably to modern diplomacy and make it a more precise and professional field.

The Precedent from Political Science

The diplomatists' problem is somewhat parallel to that of the political scientists, who, a few years ago, began research in countries in which the logic of political processes was far removed from the Western framework. They were confronted with political systems with unfamiliar assumptions about politics embedded in completely different cultures. They found differing institutions fulfilling different functions of social control and government. Leadership and leadership roles were defined in differing patterns. The traditional descriptive political science theory and procedure simply did not apply; the usual ways of posing problems and carrying out research did not work. As more new nations gained independence and as social and political development attracted more attention, the political scientists found that they needed help from the disciplines which had done the most work in the cross-cultural field. Consequently, they pragmatically turned to sister social science disciplines for the theories, conceptual approaches, and analytical methods that would apply to understanding political institutions and practices in non-Western societies.

From the cultural anthropologists they availed themselves of the *culture concept,* the outlook which sees a society's way of life as interrelated patterns of learned and shared behavior. These patterns vary enormously as different groups of humans cope with their particular social and physical environments. The dramatic contrasts between primitive societies and the developed Western world were particularly instructive. The investigator found that he should take nothing for granted in approaching the political practices of a new society. That is, he had to avoid the tendency to study the political institutions of another culture with the assumptions which would be relevant to his own—usually Western—society. The culture concept insisted that the components of culture—customs, institutions, social roles, etc.—are normally functionally interrelated and understandable only in the context of that culture. This was a useful orientation for the political scientist.

Sociology has provided political science with theory and concepts for handling the *structure and function* of institutions and of social groups. These theoretical constructs have been refined to the extent that they are subject to empirical research and to mathematical and statistical analysis; thus data can be collected and used more scientifically. From the combination of sociological and anthropological approaches, the *social system* idea was adapted to political science problems. It became the "political system" framework.

Social psychology was also sought out, often in combination with psychology-related anthropological studies, to handle contrasting value systems, perception patterns, attitudes, and habits of thinking as these factors related to political processes and institutions. Political scientists became particularly interested in the pioneering work done in the "national character" studies of the early postwar period, and have revived interest in studying culture and personality by relating this approach to political behavior.

This cross-fertilization is discussed more fully in Heinz Eulau's *The Behavioral Persuasion in Politics*.[7] The end result in political science has sometimes been described as a revolution, with the "behavioralists" challenging the traditional norms of political analysis as applied not only to the contrasting political cultures of non-Western nations but also to Western societies and even to domestic political institutions and processes. Thus Marian D. Irish stated in 1968 that "The most distinctive advance overall in American political science since World War II is its development as a basic behavioral science." [8]

The point for us is that as political scientists availed themselves of conceptual approaches from related social and psychological sciences, they greatly increased the relevancy and accuracy of political science studies conducted cross-culturally, and in the process, greatly enhanced political science as a scientific discipline. As the same time their overall methodology has become more consistent with that of the other behavioral sciences, thus facilitating interdisciplinary investigation of problems in complex modern international affairs. Now political scientists talk about political systems, political structures and functions, political roles, interest groups, value analysis, civic culture, political culture, and similar concepts related to behavioral science.

It should be noted in passing, lest the omission seem illogical, that the behavioral sciences have also made a similar impact on economics, especially on development economics. The application to economics will not be pursued very far in the chapters which follow, not because it is any less important, but because there is already considerable literature available on the subject. In any case, the interdisciplinary experience related to economics provides a less clear precedent for our purposes. Often the behavioral scientists themselves have undertaken projects related to economic matters or economic development; and on the other side of the coin, the economists have been less systematic than the political scientists in integrating behavioral concepts into their theoretical approaches.

The Core Behavioral Sciences

The parallel need for professionals in international relations and especially in public diplomacy to develop similar theoretical and conceptual capabilities is obvious. At the least, public diplomacy is the subject of *applied* social and psychological science. There is an essential difference, however: The political scientist has been concerned with building more adequate bodies of systematic theory for an academic discipline. To a large extent the behaviorally-oriented political scientist has become a behavioral scientist himself. The public diplomatist has less ambitious objectives. He does *not* intend to become a behavioral scientist; in most cases he is concerned only with increasing his ability to meet a daily round of direct and real-life problems which cut across cultural, psychological, and institutional grounds.

Making the combination of behavioral science disciplines more practically available and usable in the foreign policy and public diplomacy field involves picking and choosing from four core disciplines: sociology, cultural anthropology, social psychology, and the new political science. Our goal is to compile a reason-

ably consistent and interrelated package of practical concepts
which will require the least specialized terminology, and which
will have the most direct and obvious application to foreign
affairs problems.[9] But first some general comments regarding
these academic fields may be useful by way of orientation:

Anthropology has enjoyed a certain mystic popularity with
laymen working cross-culturally in somewhat the same way
that amateur psychiatry has enjoyed a following in some urban
social circles. Such classics as Ruth Benedict's *Patterns of Culture* (published back in 1934), or more recently Edward T.
Hall's *The Silent Language*, have become almost popular-scale
publications. Anthropologist Margaret Mead has been invited to
testify before the Senate Foreign Relations Committee—and in
fact, her name is familiar to most Western diplomats. Even
anthropological works on primitive groups and exotic cultures
have been followed rather avidly by members of the foreign
affairs community who are interested in the "natives" in their
areas of assignment. And everyone knows about "culture shock."

Actually the results of bringing anthropology to bear on
foreign affairs have been considerably less than spectacular.
There are features of anthropology as a general academic discipline which badly confuse the relationship with foreign affairs.
It began as a naturalistic, descriptive, and classifying science,
somewhat akin to biology or zoology. With such a broad field
as "man" as the subject, the subfields of anthropology have become extremely diverse. Anthropology includes, for example,
archaeology, physical anthropology, linguistics, and ethnology,
along with the more applicable social or cultural anthropology,
and certain interdisciplinary derivations such as culture and personality.

A second impediment is that the preponderant interest of
anthropologists tends to be primitive peoples and simple societies, and field methods adapted to this milieu. This interest has
been useful in administering colonial areas. The British have
used anthropologists extensively, and the United States has en-

listed their assistance in administering several of the Pacific Trust territories. But in foreign affairs, people work with few primitives. At the least foreign affairs officers work with the more sophisticated segments of the relatively traditional or tribal societies that some of the newer nations present. Only limited work has been done by anthropologists on the more complex segments of human societies, such as the urban middle classes of capital cities, or western European cultures. There are exceptions like Oscar Lewis' *Children of Sanchez*,[10] and anthropologists have studied modern peasant societies. But while these studies are relevant to certain specific interests of some foreign affairs specialists, they are marginal to much of the business of international relations. The result is that anthropology has tended to be somewhat more of an after-coffee outlet for intellectual curiosity than a serious source of concepts for foreign affairs problems or for helpful approaches to the psychological dimension of public diplomacy.

Cultural anthropology does nevertheless offer two lodes worth mining. One is the area of social or cultural anthropology (practically they mean about the same thing), which has generated theories of culture *per se* and of culture change, as was noted above when we mentioned the "culture concept." Here, in the behavioral-science orientation, the anthropologist has taken advantage of the fact that he has worked with simple and small societies. Over a period of time he has been able to observe entire societies and cultures and the full interrelation of their customs, institutions, beliefs, language, social structure, religion, etc. This has given him a unique vantage point, from which the culture concept and its related theories of society have developed. It has also offered him the opportunity of taking a comparative approach in studying human behavior, as these comprehensive studies have been done for numerous simple societies. Such comparisons highlighted the various ways in which humans can and do pattern their institutions, meet their basic and secondary needs, order and control their societies, deal with economics and exchange, and attempt to solve the rest of the problems which go with social life. Some of the concepts and theories of human behavior which resulted have been highly useful for research in such complicated human organizations as industries, armed forces, and educational institutions. They have been essential for studies of cultural change, such as the modernization of agricultural or public health methods sought in international technical assistance programs. Anthropologists have been used directly in all these endeavors.

The second lode is the product of the anthropologists' study of culture as being basically psychological behavior. That is, customs came to be seen first as shared mental habits, and culture as the group's collective knowledge, behavior expectations for the individual and for other people, beliefs and values, myths, and tendencies toward patterned anxieties, moods, and emotions. This definition followed logically from the concept that culture is learned behavior, and therefore is psychological in its transmission and practice. The result has been the *culture and personality* approach, an exceptionally useful concept for those who seek the rationale of foreign behavior, especially when contrasts in perception and reasoning are involved in international communication. These studies reached their peak in the late 1940s and early 1950s, after they were first promoted and financed as part of the war effort. Understandably, studies of Japan were especially in demand. One product was the renowned *The Chrysanthemum and the Sword* by Ruth Benedict.[11] Other studies concerned Great Britain and Germany. The United States was the subject of attention, too, as in Margaret Mead's *And Keep Your Powder Dry*.[12] The range of areas and cultures studied increased as this approach gained popularity. Unfortunately the anthropologists' interest in this endeavor has waned, as has their interest in modern and complex societies in general, particularly in recent years. Relatively little new work has been done in this field since the mid-1950s. Part of the field has been taken up by social psychologists and the new behaviorally oriented political scientists.[13]

1 / *The Relevance of the Behavioral Sciences*

Sociology's relevance to foreign affairs is also obscured by its many subdivisions. Sociology studies everything from juvenile delinquency to city planning, race relations, community organization, religion, demography, and much more. The public image of its scope is further confused by social studies which often go under the name of sociology but which are actually marginal to the field. For example, there is social philosophy, which is what sociology means in many foreign countries and from which tradition it is derived. There is also social and welfare work. Understanding of sociology as a science is also clouded by the fact that studies in sociology very properly have often been related to promoting causes or to remedial programs for societies in trouble. This was the case in American sociology particularly in the 1930s and 1940s. A variation on this theme is evident today as some sociologists choose to become activists, sometimes leaving their scientific moorings behind. There has been still another misinterpretation over the decades: Many a local elected official has confused sociology with "socialism" as he wondered what they were teaching young people down at the state university!

In a public diplomacy and foreign policy reference, we are primarily interested in what sociology has achieved as the social science with the longest experience in applying scientific methodology to the study of social groups and social institutions. It studies what they are and how they function—the structure and function of social life. Obviously sociology overlaps greatly with cultural anthropology, but it covers a narrower field, and it has moved somewhat further in the scientific mold than anthropology.

A major part of the American sociological effort goes into studying domestic problems or conditions. Most sociological research has little if any relevance to foreign affairs or policy problems. But sociologists, along with anthropologists, have worked cross-culturally, and in many cases either their research or the work of foreign sociologists working in their own countries has supplied valuable data and information pertaining to international communication. We will use sociology mainly as a resource for theory and concept which can be related to institutions and social structure.

Social psychology is often seen by cynics as the study of the human and near-human behavior of college sophomores because of the large amount of research in which professors have used their undergraduate classes as subjects. However, as it is the psychological science most concerned with the relations of the individual to the group, it is one of the most relevant when our interest is patterns of perception, opinion, attitude, and group psychological response. Its knowledge of fundamental psychological processes is based on a substantial history of scientifically respectable psychological research in a number of countries, and its network of scientific journals assures that this research adds up to a reasonably dependable resource for understanding this aspect of human behavior.

Over the last three decades, social psychologists have occasionally turned their attention to various aspects of international relations, most particularly to studies of tension and aggression as related to international conflicts, and to national perceptions and attitudes reflecting "how nations see each other." These studies are usually motivated by a desire to promote international understanding and cooperation by bringing to the surface the underlying conceptions and misconceptions which impinge on international cooperation. UNESCO sponsored some of the early projects.[14] The same approach has been used to determine the foreign image of the United States. Public opinion polls are now used for research in international politics as well as for estimating internal political situations in many countries. All these developments are highly relevant to public diplomacy and will be referred to often. Also we will use a number of conceptual approaches from social psychology.

In fact, to anticipate the following chapters, it is my belief that the best starting point for building a set of behavioral science concepts for use in foreign affairs is the social psychologist's interest in *social perception*. This element will serve as the unifying thread in the material that follows. Perception offers a number of advantages. Although it has various refined meanings in the several branches of psychology and elsewhere, these special definitions do not depart too far from the popular understanding of the word. Thus we start on familiar ground. It also expresses our key concern: How are our policy initiatives perceived, and why? A focus on perception easily allows us to "plug in" to other approaches from the behavioral sciences briefly outlined above. Questions regarding perception apply directly to international communication analysis, to the study of the effect of the press and other media on international affairs, to information programs, and to related concerns of public diplomacy.[15]

The object, then, is to develop a "behavioral science for the diplomat" with problems of public diplomacy in mind, starting with perception as the integrating concept.

II

Perceiving the Issues:

A Study in

Comparative Psychology

THE AMERICAN PUBLIC EASILY BELIEVED, AFTER the evidence was responsibly and carefully sifted, that President Kennedy's death was the murder act of one deranged person, despite rumors and publicity-seeking speculation to the contrary. Even Americans who still felt that there might have been more to the case than had come to light did not believe that any international plot or sinister design stemming from American political rivalries had been involved. Yet Americans in both official and private capacities have reported a surprisingly widespread belief abroad that a plot had been swept under the rug. Students, professional people, politicians—educated and urbane citizens—insisted that there *must* have been some political machination behind it. Then a second Kennedy was killed as he became a presidential "threat"! It is hard to tell whether our foreign friends have seen too many movies or whether they take a more cynical view of how political competition is resolved in a democratic state. But clearly there was a small, but real and patterned, difference of perception in their interpretation of the event—and of political processes in the United States. This is the kind of contrasting perception which one finds constantly in international public interpretation of events. Sometimes the difference is slight; sometimes it is so profound that there is little basis for communication.

With the public's view of international issues becoming an ever more important consideration in the deliberations of almost all nations, foreign affairs professionals must become more specific and accurate in their estimates of psychological factors on a group or even national basis. To pursue this psychological dimension, attention must be focused on two central mental processes: perception; and cognition, or less technically, the reasoning process. In other words, we need to know what and how people perceive, and then what they do with that perception—how they process it in order to respond to it. To use a computer analogy: We need to know how the public's mental computer is programmed to perceive the data available to it, and how it is programmed to process it.

In traditional diplomacy we have always been concerned with the perception and cognition patterns of identifiable individuals, usually leaders and decision makers. In public diplomacy we are more interested in typical or usual group perception and reasoning patterns. We are interested in both those patterns of which people are aware, and those which go on below the level of conscious direction. Understanding these patterns is complicated not only by international contrasts in public experience and interests but also by contrasting assumptions embedded in cultural differences.

One of the better-known cases in which contrasting perception was the subject of a policy deliberation, and one made more dramatic by wartime circumstances, was the United States' dilemma over what to do about the status of the emperor in Japan. Near the end of World War II considerable attention was given to the conditions of surrender to be demanded of the Japanese, and to the kind of regime which would follow. The part which the Emperor would play was a key issue in both.

The logical course from an American "common-sense" point of view would have been to abolish the role of the Emperor entirely, if not to punish him as a war criminal. This action would have been consistent with American deep preferences for democratic institutions, and the general feeling that it was something in the nature of the emperor-oriented Japanese government which gave rise to the Japanese military adventure in the Pacific in the first place. Further, the American point of view would expect that the Japanese people would prefer to be freed from what Americans assumed was the arbitrary authority of the Emperor. Americans would also expect that the war would have taught the Japanese a lesson about emperors. Whatever the Japanese feeling, the whole idea of emperor-style government was abhorrent to the American public, and one of the implicit ideological objectives in winning the war was to eliminate just such forms of government. Had the issue been put to a vote in the United States, the Emperor would most probably have fallen with the collapse of the Japanese military force.

This case, however, was one in which the question of perception and response—the Japanese point of view—was pursued with some sophistication and in some depth. Among other approaches, a team of behavioral scientists had been engaged in an extended project to understand Japanese rationale in wartime, and the social and psychological climate which American forces would find in occupation. These studies indicated that both the Emperor's role and the Japanese perception of it were quite different from what would be assumed without some knowledge of the Japanese collective mind. To the Japanese the Emperor was a product of national mythology, more a father image than an autocratic ruler, a symbol of the state and of the emotionally-laden value orientations which gave cohesiveness to Japanese society. In fact, it was judged that the action which would make Japanese last-ditch resistance most probable, make occupation most difficult, and tear apart Japanese social and spiritual cohesion in the difficult rehabilitation period ahead, would be just the action which seemed most indicated to the American forces—removal of the institution of the Emperor.[1]

How much the studies by the specialists affected the decision is not entirely clear. In any case, the United States was persuaded that it was in the interest of an early Japanese surrender and also of the occupying forces after surrender to retain the Emperor. The new Japanese constitution subsequently called on him to renounce the religious definition of his status, and otherwise adjusted his role to a more democratic society. But the Emperor remained, and from the vantage point of twenty-five years later, few qualified observers would argue that a mistake had been made.

In this instance, making an estimate of the psychological forces involved was relatively simple. The question was clear-cut. It was not too hard for the Americans to appreciate the fact that the Japanese would think differently on such matters, given the obvious contrast in cultures. A patterned willingness to undertake suicide bombing missions, among other things, had already indicated a substantial psychological gulf between the United States and Japan. And a number of area experts were available to add weight to the extensive research which had been conducted on the issue. The Japanese dilemma illustrates rather dramatically a reality present in some degree in most international communication; that is, that just as perception and cognition differ from person to person, so do they differ in a demonstrable way from one society to another. It is the purpose of this chapter, then, to seek a basis for working with the *group-* and *national-level* psychological factors involved in international affairs.

Perception, Cognition, and Personality

Let us start with the commonly held understanding of our subject: Perception and reasoning are highly individualistic matters. We are aware that no two people see even the most everyday event from exactly the same point of view, nor do they evaluate and respond to events in the same way. There is always some difference in individual experience, mood, or knowledge, which provides a unique mental predisposition from which each person views or hears of events. We know from extensive psychological experimentation that it is quite possible for people to "see" elements in an event which were not actually there. It is also apparent that no one ever perceives all that there is to perceive. People perceive very selectively and according to the particular complex of interests and concerns which characterizes their individual mental set of the moment.

Conversely, people are *selectively inattentive.* They allow large quantities of potential stimuli to pass them by, from the traffic noise in the street to people passing directly in front of them. Sometimes selective perception is more or less consciously controlled, as when scanning the morning paper—no one reads every article. Usually the selection process goes on in the cerebral cortex without our awareness or conscious direction. The more one thinks of the multiplicity of factors which can influence perception the more impressed one must be with the complexity of the neural processes which go on in the human brain. Even at the age of one year, an infant's experience is sufficiently varied to provide a vast number of independent variables in his perception system; by adulthood the situation appears impossibly complex. It is easy to appreciate the popular notion that human behavior is beyond the reach of scientific understanding.

Much of what we do know about perception processes is based on experiments in visual or auditory perception of physical objects, sounds, drawings, etc., which might be perceived in varying contexts or spatial relationships, or under varying psychological conditions. Also many experiments have been made in socially defined situations or in the presence of other people so that factors in interpersonal relationships, suggestion, prejudice, and similar items could be experimentally examined for their influence on perception. This background is extensively reviewed in many textbooks and readers in psychology.[2] Much of what is reported from these experiments does not come as a surprise or as particularly mysterious phenomena since these findings would generally correspond to our own experience, at least when the process is called to our attention.

For the present discussion, it is necessary to reduce the complexity of individual perception and cognition to more manageable abstractions which can be applied to group perception and thus to international communication and public diplomacy analysis. To do this we move on to the concept of *personality*, then to patterns in personality, and finally to the relationship between personality patterns and social experience or culture.

Personality as a "Psychological World"

We may simplify what we have said above by saying that every individual lives simultaneously in two worlds—the world of reality; and his own psychological, or, more precisely, cognitive world. The world of "reality" (a concept that might itself set off a philosophical argument) surrounds the individual with an environment composed of real physical objects, events, other people doing describable things for presumably objectively describable motives, and even more abstract entities such as communities and nations. A person's psychological world, on the other hand, includes much which is not present in the immediate world of reality—knowledge, memory, fantasy, beliefs, anxieties, and so forth.[3]

These two worlds overlap somewhat, but it is obvious that they do not coincide. There is a vast range of items in the world of reality which does not exist in one's psychological world, for one cannot be aware of everything. Unaided by observational tools, the human is confined to the limits of his sensory equipment; most people cannot hear sounds above 16,000–18,000 cycles per second, for example. There are people whose psychological worlds do not include germs, cosmic radiation, or the United States.

The structure of the psychological world is particularly interesting. Past events can persist in memory, even in a kind of memory transmitted from a previous generation. Future events exist in expectations, along with purely imaginary events in day-dreams. Potential calamities exist in inner fears and anxieties. We can experience vicariously and add to our psychological worlds the vast variety of other people's experiences through the symbolism of written and spoken words. We can "see" indirectly through photographs or art or television. We can deal in abstractions. We can think up new things or events and even communicate them to the psychological worlds of other people without any evidence that they ever did or will exist in any world of reality. Such is the potential of the human mind.

One evidence of this phenomenon is the familiar Rorschach, or ink-blot test. The subject is presented with a series of abstract figures formed by pressing a bit of ink in a fold of paper. The resulting ink blots assume shape and texture at random, and of course carry no meaning. The subject is asked to talk about the figures and describe what he sees in them, and why. Form, texture, and contrasts in the ink blots come to life as the subject's psychological world is projected onto the blots to produce butter-flies, dragons, mothers-in-law, or wine glasses. It has been reported that once when the test was given in the Middle East, an Arab subject said matter of factly that he saw an ink blot, but usually psychologists claim that the test, properly used, yields some insight into the organization of a subject's psychological world.

To understand how perception is a function of the psycholog-ical world several of its properties should be noted. We have al-ready indicated that content is of paramount importance, but more than content is involved, for all sane individuals have psy-chological worlds which are organized, structured, and meaningful. Specific knowledge, remembered experience, acquired drives and anxieties, basic assumptions, prejudices, and all the rest which make up a cognitive structure serve the individual well only if the various elements are reasonably consistent with each other and with the environmental situations with which the individual must normally deal. Otherwise one would have a hopeless task of focusing one's thinking in sufficiently consistent patterns to produce the constancy in behavior necessary to carry out essential tasks or to make one's behavior predictable to the people with whom one must interact. The psychotic personality is one which by organic malfunction or by functional distortion has lost the ability to maintain this minimum adaptive consistency. And conversely, there seems to be a relationship between the amount of strain to which the personality is subjected in the course of coping with a modern complex or contradictory environment and the incidence of functional psychosis.

Therefore, the adaptive function of the personality is to maintain its integration and internal meaning. As a result, people are most inclined to perceive new events or experiences in a way which will disturb the existing organization as little as possible. For example, in several Far East cultures, giggling and even laughing are signs of embarrassment or anxiety. This behavior has understandably created perception problems for Westerners: In wartime, prisoners were given harsh treatment for lack of respect, tourists have noted what gay, fun-loving people Orientals are, and technical advisors have wished their counterparts would be more serious about the business at hand.

One will try to fit that which is new into the existing complex of past experience, knowledge, prejudice, or belief. The truth or the honest motive will not be perceived as such if the source is suspect or is believed to have reasons to distort the facts. On the other hand, patently absurd statements or an obviously illogical explanation of, let us say, a policy decision, can be uncritically and even enthusiastically accepted if it blends easily with existing beliefs and habits of reasoning. This is not necessarily justice, but it is sound psychology. It applies to an American's perception of a foreign policy as well as to a foreign public's perceptions of American intentions. And it applies to communication between a government and its own people.

Peace Corps volunteers frequently have had difficulty explaining themselves in host communities abroad where the idea of the Peace Corps, and the volunteers' appearance, habits, and motives are all foreign to the experience and understanding of local citizens. It is a situation calling for a "logical" explanation, and local critics often supply it: The strangers are agents of the C.I.A. The community may not have a very clear idea of the C.I.A. either, but will have heard of it and have some image of it—usually highly distorted. So the charge makes some sense, and a native "explanation" is more to be trusted than a foreign one. Consequently, the volunteers have an uphill struggle turning perceptions around.

This internal organization of the individual's psychological world also tends to determine what a person chooses—consciously or not—to perceive, and what to ignore. One is tuned to notice that which meshes meaningfully with the elements and organization of one's cognitive processes, and to pass over that which does not, at least until the strength of the stimulus is overpowering. Thus a well-traveled urban elite may be attentive to daily foreign affairs issues while a more provincial small-town citizen or farmer may not.

Moreover, since one does not usually observe items in one's environment in their totality or "from all sides," one tends to provide one's own meaning and interpretation on the basis of one's own "larger picture," i.e., the content and structure of one's own psychological world.[4] For example, I was present in the small city of Ormoc in the Philippines when a U.S. destroyer made the first goodwill visit in twenty years. Considerable naval action had taken place there during World War II. The first problem was to convince the populace that new warfare was not imminent.

Perception becomes more complicated in modern or changing societies where the individual's cognitive world necessarily is less simply and easily integrated. Compare the urban businessman with a peasant farmer. Here especially we may find what has been described as "cognitive dissonance," or a psychological world in which the elements are not comfortably consistent and integrated.[5] Thus we have a more unstable perception situation and one more likely to be inconsistent, or susceptible to change. Ambivalent feelings lead to ambivalent perceptions; the same person perceives in differing patterns under differing circumstances. Newly presented events or ideas may increase the dissonance, or may help resolve it, leading to changes in cognitive organization. Or, in simpler communication terms, a change in "point of view" may result. When we bring visitors to the United States under our various cultural exchange programs, we presumably choose candidates whose minds are not yet fully closed —i.e., cognitive dissonance regarding the United States exists. We then hope that an actual visit will help resolve this dissonance in favor of a more sympathetic or at least a more objective basis for future perceptions of the U.S. and American activities. It does not always work out that way, as many a cultural affairs officer can testify. The dissonance is sometimes resolved in a still more prejudiced direction, with the resulting judgments being strengthened and validated by firsthand experience. These are the pitfalls when we try to make someone change his mind.

The important point in all this is that in order to understand how people perceive events and issues in international affairs and to understand how they respond to these perceptions it is necessary to comprehend the psychological or cognitive worlds of the people involved—the content, the internal organization, the amenability to change, the emotional strength of beliefs. We will refer back to this framework of analysis, always stressing that how people perceive is not determined by how they *should* perceive, from an objective definition of a situation, but how in fact they *do* perceive, as determined by the content and organization of their particular psychological worlds. It is useless to bemoan the fact that people can and often do perceive on the basis of totally false premises, from erroneous information, or from many combinations of rumor, hearsay, or faulty memory. And it is equally useless to suppose that their perception can be greatly improved by pointing out the error of their ways. The communications analyst's "real world" includes the usually unreal psychological worlds of the communications audience.

Now let us go back to the case of interpreting Japanese perceptions of and responses to the role of their Emperor. Note that we were referring to *generalized* Japanese perceptions, that is, the perceptions of a whole nation rather than of specific individuals. Let us examine the extent to which we can go beyond our earlier statement that perception and response are highly individualistic matters. If we could establish a basis for typical or "normal" perception patterns for large groups of people, even nations, the cause of public diplomacy would be greatly advanced. The question then is: To what extent do people who share a given national experience and identity, or a common culture, develop similarities in private cognitive worlds and therefore provide a basis for describing a collective pattern of perception habits and reasoning processes? This field of investigation is usually referred to as *culture and personality* studies, or less precisely, national character studies.

Culture and Personality

Personality, without being too technical about it, is the internal psychic organization of one's ideas, emotions, knowledge, likes and dislikes, prejudices, habits of logic, values, etc., which tends to act as the filter through which one perceives the world and its events, and which in turn serves as a censor to select and direct responses to whatever stimuli are perceived. This is another, more exact, way of saying psychological world. Just how this mental process works remains an intriguing scientific question; much highly sophisticated work has and is being done on the functions of the brain and on the intricate physiological processes involved. For public diplomacy purposes, it is more practical to concentrate on the more comprehensible level of how personality and personality formation work out in observable behavior. If we know something about an individual's personality, we are much better equipped to predict how he will respond in given circumstances. If common personality patterns could be described for groups of people, it might be possible to make better predictions as to how national groups would respond to particular policy initiatives, to international events, to news coverage, or to another nation's actions. We recognize that there exists a typical French anxiety regarding German intentions near France's borders, due to the history of European conflicts; or that typical Latin American images of the United States contribute to national-level reactions to "imperialism" or "economic aggression."

When we examine the factors which lead to the formation of any normal individual's personality structure, we can distinguish three general categories of determinants which explain both the uniqueness of each personality and the basis for group personality patterns.[6]

Physical characteristics. People vary in such attributes as cerebral capacity, glandular function, resistance to disease, strength, and basic metabolism. It is reasonable to suppose that such differences affect personality and account for some of the variations in personality among individuals. But physical factors seem to provide very little basis for determining group personality patterns. Physical factors associated with racial distinctions, particularly, have no scientifically demonstrable effect on personality. (Racial factors in a social setting are another matter.) Although genetic research is continuing, scientists tell us that the biological equipment normally found in any racial group is consistent with any of the varied personality patterns found in human society. There appears to be no irregular distribution of built-in instincts. But the variation in psychological makeup which can result from differing learning processes in various cultures is enormous.[7] Cases abound in history and legend in which a child of one race grew up with another and assumed the culture, life style, and personality of the foster society. Frances Slocum of American pioneer stock was raised among the Indian tribes of Indiana, and as an adult was almost indistinguishable from the Indians. An infant of American missionary parentage abandoned during a Chinese revolution and raised as a Chinese peasant came to live, talk, and think so much like the Chinese peasants that he resisted repatriation later in life. The socializing process in the American melting pot has produced personality patterns fully in the mold of American life, far removed from those of the parent culture. So, despite Nazi insistence, we assign the biological determinant to the realm of explaining differences among individual personalities, not to psychological differences or similarities among either ethnic or racial groups.

Individualized experience. No two people, even identical twins, go through identical life experiences, or go through them in the same sequence, or under the same emotional conditions. Here again we have a basis for variation in personality formation, and especially for the differences to which we are most attuned within our own society. For it is in knowing these personal differences among our associates that we are able to empathize informally and predict or anticipate individualized reactions and responses. But because we focus so much of our attention on this aspect of the individuality of personality, we fail to see that there is also a great amount of *shared* experience which goes into the personality formation process.

Socially shared and culturally transmitted experience. Here we find the basis on which people who share a common way of life develop a certain similarity of personality. Or let us say that people's personalities, by being composed largely of learned wisdom and attitude, acquired appetites, anxieties, and all the rest, tend to be consistent with the idea patterns and mental customs which are culturally transmitted and even socially demanded, and which fit into the "common sense" of the society in question. American society provides a difficult case study because it is complex, mobile, and is still composed of many ethnic groups. Still, it is normal, for example, to have been reared in a nuclear family with two to four children. If an American today has ten brothers and sisters plus several other relatives in the household, he recognizes that his family life falls in the range of nontypical or individualized experience. American children receive relatively similar care in infancy; they attend schools with remarkably similar curricula. They watch the same television programs from coast to coast, are buffeted by the same advertising, and identify with American society's heroes and heroic events—ranging from baseball and the entertainment world to statesmen and military leaders. They internalize from the society certain notions of ethical behavior, which, while changing and not always consistent, nevertheless provide in cross-cultural perspective a typical American judgment of right and wrong, sanctioned behavior and disapproved behavior. Through literature, the editorial pages, even through the comics, Americans are subtly exposed to the conventional morality of the society. Even when it is debated in detail the main assumptions remain when compared cross-culturally.

Neither experience nor thought patterns are static—the values of a group do change. The McGuffey reader was a recognized and shared common reading experience a few generations ago, as were Horatio Alger books and Zane Grey's Western novels. Today the morality of rugged individualism expressed in these sources has somewhat given way to a morality more consistent with an individual's need to adjust and cooperate with groups in a more diversified society. One of the more explicit statements of this shift was made in David Riesman's *The Lonely Crowd*.[8] Another well-known commentary is William H. White's *The Organization Man*.[9] Still, when these changes are seen against the wide range of cultures around the world, they become only variations on a theme, and the American's ethic as an individual in his society retains a certain uniqueness even while changing.

Growing up in America exposes one to the high value placed on time, efficiency, and progress; on entrepreneurship and productivity; on applied knowledge and science; and on the wealth of appliances and gadgets which science can produce. This orientation has much to do with economic life. From childhood one hears of the public interest, the will of the majority, the voting process and its consequences on local and national life. The child sees group problems typically attacked by committees of all kinds in all segments of life. He thus gains certain assumptions and outlooks which are basic to American political life and to the American outlook on political life in other countries.

American society presents an all-pervading emphasis on achievement, its value, and the rewards which go with it. In cross-cultural perspective, the American is optimistic, and believes in happy endings, which result from the application of human effort and tenacity. It is a problem-solving, activistic society. This motif has been at the foundation of American behavior from the conquering of the frontier to the placing of a man on the moon.

Being socialized into American life exposes one to the American concept of social relations, the middle-class orientation, the egalitarian ideal, informality in personal relationships, mobility in changing friendships and loyalties. Thus we have a basis, despite difficulties, for describing an American pattern of personality associated with American experience and culture.

Latin America also is a highly heterogeneous area with sharp urban-rural contrasts adding to the otherwise implanted cultural variations. Its culture is essentially in the Western tradition, yet certain patterned variations in personality or in the content and structure of the Latin American psychological world stand in contrast to the United States. In Latin America the growing child is more likely to be socialized in a larger immediate family, made even larger by a broader recognition of blood relatives and a series of ceremonial relatives on the periphery (e.g., "padrino," or godfather). From the beginning his social world consists of differing emotional ties and distinct concepts of the relationship between the individual and his group and of reciprocal responsibilities to other people. The Latin American child is much less likely to be presented with an integrated configuration of middle-class values. What middle classes exist are small in number, relatively new, ill-defined, and largely limited to metropolitan centers. The larger social world consists mostly of a high-status elite or pretending elite on the one hand, and a peasantry or self-acknowledged working class on the other, and tends to mold the pattern of one's expectations regarding life style and position in the society. Traditionally the conception of the individual's relationship to his environment has a strong fatalistic element; life and its circumstances are more typically seen as given. The individual's task is to adjust to rather than to manipulate the world about him. If one is to change things, one more typically appeals to the larger forces, which are seen as the controlling agents—the divine, the government, perhaps the *patron*. Fate is often the central theme of literature, art, and the movies. Individualism is a function of personal dignity and its protection, rather than of the self-reliant achievement orientation born on the United States frontier. Friendship has a more formal and ceremonial expression. Great value is placed on argumentation and debate; the idea is often valued more than the practical application.[10]

Culture is changing in Latin America, of course; values are shifting—and at a very fast pace in recent years. But in cross-cultural perspective these changes, like those in the United States and elsewhere, are variations on a theme. The person socialized in the mainstream of Latin American culture is still exposed to a unique combination of ideas and attitudes, which logically results in patterns of personality which in the typical case would differ in important respects from those of North America—or of Japan, Germany, or China under the Communist regime.

35)

We see from these examples that in the process of experiencing the everyday events of one's society and having pressed upon one the beliefs and assumptions of other people, one tends to internalize a pattern of personality suggested by that society. In fact, the most basic service rendered by a society is to provide a set of pretested ways to think, believe, evaluate, and understand what is accepted behavior and what is not. While individuals are allowed to assume unique personality characteristics to a degree, the culture sets the limits. And the society expects, even demands, that its members internalize the general pattern as a matter of course if they are to interact smoothly with other members of the society, participate in its institutions, or take advantage of the package of common sense provided so that they will not have to go through a laborious decision-making process whenever a choice of action or behavior is called for.

The mental customs which make up personality can become very detailed, indeed; for all specific customs, such as eating with a fork rather than chopsticks, or speaking one's language, are, in the final analysis, habits in the mind, where actions are selected and controlled. It follows that culture is also a psychological phenomenon in the final analysis. Therefore, no matter how individualistic a person may think he is, the chances are that most of his thoughts, from his choice of breakfast food to what he wants the government to do, are shaped by his culture.

This phenomenon is what the cultural anthropologists and the social psychologists are driving at when they talk about the relationship between culture and personality. The terminology for it has varied. "Basic personality structure" has been used, particularly when the psychiatrists interested themselves in the subject, and became concerned with typical fundamental aspects of personality organization, such as might be manifested in emotions or styles of personality integration. "Theme" has been used when trying to isolate key value orientations or belief structures which appear to describe the essential qualities of group personality patterns and in turn help explain secondary thought habits. The term most often used has been "national character," which has the broadest meaning of all. It gained currency with the expansion of studies in this field during and immediately after World War II, when the specific objective was to understand personality factors on a national basis. Unfortunately, the term presents problems. "National" is often too general and even appears superficial in complex societies in which regional or important subcultural distinctions need to be recognized. "Character" is also misleading; it is too easily used to describe the quality or style of the actions of the nation state itself or its government rather than the shared personality patterns of the society.[11] For example, this connotation is possible in describing the English resistance to the Axis in World War II as "English perseverance."

More recently the behavioral scientists have favored "modal personality," a concept which suggests greater statistical accuracy and is more applicable to complex societies, where thought patterns are not homogeneous and where several "modes" of thought about a given subject may occur in a frequency distribution. This term implies that certain personality patterns may appear with exceptional frequency, but not uniformly. The idea of modal personality applies easily to studying subgroups in a society, or particular interest groups.[12]

Of all these terms, modal personality probably best fits the conceptual scheme which we have developed in this chapter. It also appears more sensible for application to the field of foreign affairs, although "national character" is more descriptive and better known. If we keep in mind that national character is composed of typical or usual personality traits found in groups of people who have shared a common experience and therefore tend to perceive and reason in similar ways, the term may be the choice one for the foreign affairs specialist. "National character" will be so understood when used in this and in following chapters. Whatever it is called, this appreciation of the relationship between culture and personality is one of the most important conceptual tools from the behavioral science field for comprehending the nature of the perception and response dimension of public diplomacy. While it would be desirable to have finished research already compiled on the major culture areas of the world, unfortunately the tool is more available than the finished descriptive products.

It is especially important for the foreign affairs specialist to become comfortable with this concept, for clearly applicable professional studies on the subject of his immediate interest will not usually be available, and he will have to come to his own conclusions regarding the predominant modes of thought and bases for perception which apply to his problem. The concept at least clarifies what one is looking for. But it cannot be emphasized too strongly that although humans are brothers physically they are *not* necessarily fundamentally alike in their "human nature" when thought and perception processes are concerned. Neither are personality types distributed at unpredictable random. Personality is a function of the social and cultural nature of human life, and perception and cognitive process follow culturally-related patterns which can be described and predicted.

We do, in fact, informally describe and predict such matters with greater or less accuracy all the time when dealing with foreign peoples. One expects a British diplomatic colleague, for example, to be somewhat more reserved in manner, perhaps less excitable in discussion, and more articulate than, let us say, his Italian counterpart. Americans think of Germans as placing more value on well-defined authority than Americans do, and perhaps more on precision. Everyone has heard about "face" in the Orient. So such images normally do enter into the thinking of diplomats and policy makers in the routine of international affairs. The problem is to become much more sophisticated and accurate in analysis, and consequently more accurate in interpretation and prediction.

The task is complicated because there are several levels of abstraction on which thought patterns may relate to perception.

Sometimes the simplest bits of behavior are involved. For example, Hall has pointed out that one's emotional and psychological equanimity can be upset by the way that space and time are handled in differing cultures.[13] Standing too close to an American during a conversation can create a clash of feeling which can confuse perception and leave the American so uncomfortable about the speaker's intentions that the substance of the conversation is all but lost. The differing meanings of a gesture can set off a series of misperceptions. In South Asia, pointing the soles of one's shoes toward a visitor, as when relaxing with one's feet on the desk, is a rudeness that is hard to excuse. Repugnance toward what is interpreted as a violation of manners, moral principles, or religious tenets can interfere enormously with the communication process. Americans in developing countries have real difficulty working with counterparts who they know are supplementing meager official salaries with the petty graft the local system allows.

At the upper end of the range of abstraction are such questions as how ideas are interconnected in patterns of logic— whether, for example, reasoning follows an inductive and practical approach for "seeing the problem" in the style of Galileo, or a model of deductive reasoning in the style of Aristotle. Somewhere in between on the range of abstraction, whole systems of idea patterns underlie perception, as in a religious system like Islam, or in the rationale of the capitalistic system.

Further, there is the problem of taking nonobjective or nonrational idea patterns seriously. Groups, like individuals, may hold ideas and beliefs contrary to objective reality or inconsistent with scientific observation, as we have pointed out. Or beliefs may not be provable one way or the other. There is such a great variety of beliefs about afterlife among the various cultures of the world that one, if not all of them, must be wrong. Yet it is the *fact* of the belief not the correctness which is decisive. And if the group holds the belief, delusion though it may be, the group supports the individual in holding that belief. It is the man with private delusions who upsets things. Perhaps the reader recalls the explanation of the difference between the psychotic and the neurotic. The psychotic believes that two and two are five—his ideas on the matter exceed the tolerance of his group, so he is a bit psychotic. The neurotic agrees that two and two are four, but he worries about it! This definition is quite consistent with the national character idea. You can worry about your group's beliefs and take positions near the limits of your culture, but if you agree when the chips are down that two and two are four, or recognize that other people believe they are four, you are normal and your wisdom is conventional.

One way to study national character with some degree of order is to seek out central value orientations (or "themes," as noted above) which are not only important in themselves, but which also help define the quality and meaning of a succession of other characteristic thought patterns which are interrelated to the central value orientation. An example in American society is the value placed on achievement. Even though it seems inconsistent with some of the actual conditions of American life, and even though this value orientation is changing to some extent, for the outside observer it remains a convenient point of entry into American national character or modal personality systems. Achievement and all the attendant thought patterns which have surrounded it permeate and determine the logic of our personal lives, our community activities, our economic and productive system, our social prestige system, and our form of democratic political practice. It leads to an appreciation of competition in American society and of the value placed on work and applied knowledge.

Social psychologist David McClelland and his associates have gained some fame by suggesting that, with some variation, Americans acquire from their society a particular psychological need to achieve, and that this need has much to do with understanding American entrepreneurship and its effect on American life.[14] Further studies by the same researchers indicate that such an acquired need is not present to the same degree in all cultures or over periods of time. Obviously, such an element in American personality patterns would be an important factor in the development of the American economy. The presence or absence of this psychological mainspring in other cultures might constitute a new dimension in the economic development problem. If it is missing in the basic drives and motivation patterns in less developed countries, one would have to question whether entrepreneurship can play the role in development which it has in the United States. If it cannot, then some basic assumptions about development abroad are disturbed. If a need to achieve is missing, but essential, can it be introduced in a society? And can it be introduced in less than the several generations which would normally be required for substantial changes to take place in core value systems? McClelland has tried to do so on an experimental scale in several countries, especially India. He reports numerous problems, and some success.[15]

The achievement motif can explain certain problems in international communication. The American is frequently charged with being materialistic. This accusation upsets him. He recognizes that he is blessed with many material items he considers necessities but which others must consider luxuries. He has a distinct emotional attachment to a high standard of living and may boast about it indiscreetly. Yet he feels misunderstood, and cannot concede that he is the boorish character implied, that he is without civilized traditions or humanistic values. The difficulty is that material possessions and the use of them have a *social meaning* which escapes the foreign critic: Material possessions are, in large part, symbols of achievement, both personal and national, and may be more important to the owner in this context than for their more obvious practical or luxury use. This "social symbol" aspect often goes astray even within American society, of course, but in cross-cultural perspective, the critic will not understand American so-called materialism unless he understands the achievement motif in some depth. Thus differences in value orientation can help explain communication breakdowns. In this case, if the critic comes from a society in which the enjoyment of material goods is confined to wealthy elites, or to a new rich whose methods of acquisition are more exploitation than personal achievement, it is understandable that he misreads the signals from the American. For, after all, value systems are much less visible than automobiles or expensive tape recorders.

In the Philippines, one of the central value systems which goes far in explaining the rationale of national life, including politics and business, is the salient concern with reciprocity, with particularly high value placed on properly honoring obligations. The good life is seen as living in a secure human network in which one is bound, and protected, by obligations. Thus a local villager thinks it only proper to vote for the politician whose influence directed public works funds in that village's direction, or perhaps provided jobs, for the villager has entered into a reciprocal responsibility. Many salient Philippine cultural patterns involve techniques for remembering details of the reciprocity net, and for fulfilling reciprocal demands. In Japan a similar but much more elaborated concept of obligation and debt explains much of Japanese behavior, even to the proper use of suicide. Family relations, labor and management affairs, respect for the Emperor, all have intricate definitions of assuming and discharging personal obligation. The Japanese language is endowed with numerous complicated honorifics to be used in address and in paying deference, which imply degrees and kinds of mutual obligation. This makes the language especially difficult for Westerners, for not only must they learn the basic honorifics, but the logic behind them—and this becomes the most "foreign" part of the language.

National character, like individual personality, must have a certain degree of internal consistency. Thus identifying core value orientations is particularly helpful in understanding the other attitudes, beliefs, acquired needs, and acquired anxieties which must be generally consistent with the core value orientations.

Let us summarize the implications for foreign affairs. The course which a modern international relations issue takes depends more and more on the way in which international events and proposed arrangements are perceived by the national publics involved, how these publics reason about what they perceive, and how they are motivated to respond. As this perception and reasoning involve a collective psychological world, a government's position on an issue is influenced by the pattern of personality content and organization of the groups which make up the politically active and articulate part of the population, or perhaps of the entire nation. Attention to national character or elements of modal personality is therefore essential if we wish to understand all the dynamics of international relations.

III

Differing Points of View

below the National Surface

WHEN WE ACTUALLY GET DOWN TO WORK IN THE public dimension of foreign policy problems, we need to take a nation apart, figuratively, to see what makes its collective perception and reasoning processes tick. Rarely is a government's policy position the resultant of a single-minded nationwide interest or view. Hence, one must usually attempt to capture the mentality of significant groups rather than of the entire population, and attempt to determine how opinions of component groups are formed and brought to bear on national decision making. This approach is important in understanding a nation as a communication system, and in communicating directly with specific groups within a foreign society. Since in both processes, the "position" which groups of people occupy in their society has much to do with their perception of public and international affairs, it is essential that we understand how contrasts in social structure can affect patterns of perception. Routinely, of course, one must also understand the thinking of specific individuals occupying specific jobs and social positions. Status and role concept is very useful here, and will be examined later in the chapter.

A Nation as a Communication System

As most foreign policy decisions in most countries have a public dimension, decisions are, in part, functions of the nature of a nation's communication system, and especially of its *political* communication system. In a cybernetics kind of process, each new governmental decision is influenced by domestic feedback from interested groups reacting to new information as well as to previous decisions. Decisions accordingly are readjusted and redirected to accommodate the public's view of the issues. Much of the new work in comparative politics is concerned with this process.

By now most political scientists working cross-culturally have adopted a vocabulary which includes such items as "interest groups," "interest articulation," "interest aggregation," and similar concepts.[1] Or they speak with increasing familiarity of elites, bureaucracies, the military, entrepreneurs, middle sectors, peasant leagues—all terms which demonstrate that the psychology of political behavior is a function of social structure and of interest-group divisions communicating and interacting within the national political system.[2]

These social structure approaches have expanded the analytical horizons of political science very substantially. As we have said, political science no longer depends simply on the traditional descriptive and historical approach which tends to impose the conventional Western conceptualization of political processes on the new and changing social and political systems of non-Western nations. It recognizes that the entire rationale for political institutions or for the use of political power may differ as the society, its institutions, social structure, and cultural base differ. The new structure-function and behavioralist concepts have led the political scientists to a fresh examination of the interest groups which are significant in any particular political system. And they can differ remarkably. In Southeast Asia Buddhist monks are a significant counter in the political game, as are the winegrowers in France, the Palestine guerillas in Jordan, or —as a more unusual example—the *Iglesia ni Cristo* sect in the Philippines. Less exclusive attention is focused on the formal structures of government, and more heed is paid to determinants found in the informal processes of political life. The political scientist's quest inevitably involves the social matrix of the society as he determines what each group's concerns are and how they are "articulated," "aggregated," and "communicated." Since a nation is a communication system, the political system is understandable only in these terms.

Obviously, to understand a nation as a communication system one must know something of the forms of communication used and how they function. Television, the press, interpersonal communication, and rumor are all potential parts of the network. Popular conceptions regarding which sources of news can be trusted, the customary means of persuasion, access to information from outside the country and the credence given it, and the effect of movies or more subtle forms of communication can be important. Other writers have explored these vital aspects of a national communication system.[3] In this chapter we will concentrate less on the political dynamics of communication and more on how to analyze a nation's social structure in order to provide a framework for differentiating patterns of perception and reasoning. Social structure runs the gamut from identifying distinct ethnic groups in a national population down to the micro level of status and role.

"People-to-People" Communication

A great deal of the communication related to international affairs takes place directly between a group in one country and its counterpart in another. Or, a government will have international programs which involve communicating with specific groups in another country. Thus there is a need to know how identifiable groups of people perceive in differing patterns, just as at the national level one tries to account for differences in national character. For example, military groups of one country work with those of another; businessmen interact with their foreign counterparts; university students and professors engage in international exchange programs. The task, therefore, is to capture the varying mentalities of significant groups within a nation.[4]

One interest group which frequently assumes importance in foreign affairs deliberations is labor—as a human resource, as an ever-present factor in economic affairs, or more often as a political force. In almost every country labor has become a major interest group which the government must take into account. As an organized political force it has formed the very basis of government from Great Britain to Peron's Argentina. Its interests have served as the basis for fundamental ideological changes in governments, with obvious consequences for international relations. The United Nations International Labor Office has been in existence longer than the United Nations itself. Even outside government channels, international labor movements have produced an increasing impact on international communication and interaction.

Accordingly, a number of nations, as a matter of international policy, have sought to influence the international labor field. The threat of such efforts by Communist states has become a matter of deep concern in some Western circles. The United States government contributes to the American Institute for Free Labor Development, joining with U.S. labor organizations and with management to promote modern democratic labor movements in the developing world. Less official organizations also have entered the international labor field. From West Germany encouragement goes to a form of the Christian Democratic labor movement; and some units of the Catholic Church have an interest in international labor programs.

Certain built-in differences exist in basic assumptions, self-images, and points of view between American labor unions and their European counterparts. (In the case of labor groups in the developing world, the differences have been sharper, and communication even more difficult.) European and American labor have differing basic conceptions of labor as a political organization, of the role of labor in sharing ownership and management of productive enterprises, and even of labor as a potential revolutionary group whose objective might be to control a state by force. One has only to recall recent British Labour governments, the real appeal of Communism to some European labor groups, or the part which labor played in Mussolini's Italy or Hitler's Germany.

Part of the difference can be explained by the differing social structures from which European and American labor movements have developed. The European worker's basic assumptions stem from a more tightly stratified society, which still survives in many parts of Europe. Even English society, to which American society is similar in many respects, retains an aura of stratification not found in the United States. Hence European workers have tended to identify themselves, their interests, and their fortunes more closely with labor as a class and as a homogeneous interest group. The European worker is more likely to see his advantage in labor's winning greater power as a group in government, or even by overthrowing the "exploiting" classes above them. There is less reason to aspire to get ahead *individually;* at least there is less precedent in habits of thought to suggest doing so than is the case in the United States. The difference is getting smaller, but it remains real.

The American laborer, regardless of his actual situation in the American industrialized society, tends to retain more of the thinking and assumptions of the individualist, joins labor movements less enthusiastically even today, and cherishes his personal political independence. His standard of living is high, and his participation in the nation's productivity is relatively higher than the European's. He may own stocks himself. Even if he does not anticipate much social and economic advancement for himself, in the American middle-class tradition he thinks it possible for his children. He is less inclined to see an advantage in overthrowing the system. In 1970, the "hard hats" showed little sympathy toward students who would challenge the establishment.

It is evident from these contrasting social structures that there are substantial reasons for differences in perception and in basic assumptions when labor groups are compared cross-culturally. These differences must be anticipated as one observes the international labor scene or attempts to construct international policies and programs. It is interesting to note that some American labor specialists find that in training Latin American labor leaders for more effective roles in a democratic society, it is better to send them to England or to Western Europe than to the United States. Communication is enhanced when the social structure and the assumptions about society and government are more alike.

Social Structure and Perception

Social structure is, of course, the subject matter of sociology, at least to the extent that lines can be drawn to divide disciplines in the behavioral sciences. To apply the national character concept of Chapter II to understanding subgroups within the national society, one must know something of the psychological implications of social stratification. The sociological approach is basic also to understanding the "modal personality" of national societies, for value orientations and specific perception and reasoning patterns tend to cluster around particular segments of the society whose members tend to be more homogeneous in their shared experience, daily problems, and sense of personal identity within the society. Thus members of such American societal subdivisions as the managerial or executive professions will have something of a subcultural "character" which will be distinguishable from that of school teachers or of small businessmen.

In short, in social perception, people will have differing points of view according to the position in the social structure from which they perceive events, just as people perceive physical objects or events in unique ways according to their particular position in space and their distance from the objects or events. Some differences in social perception involve ethnic identity and varying degrees of effective participation in national or international affairs. Other pertinent differences involve class divisions, especially the evolving new middle sectors of developing societies. And contrasting outlooks which go with differing definitions of status and role are important considerations in cross-cultural communication. These several aspects of social structure will be considered separately.

Ethnic and Subcultural Diversity

In order to apply terms like national character or modal personality to a total national society, we have to assume a sufficiently homogeneous culture to provide the basis for national level personality patterns and common perception habits. Then the obvious question is to what extent does a nation, in fact, share a common culture. Factors such as size, ethnic diversity, and amount of communication all play a part. Sometimes regional or certain special interest groups are sufficiently different that while fundamentally they share the national culture, they can be described as a variant on the theme, or a "subculture." All these factors affect the extent to which there is a typical national point of view or consensus regarding an international issue. The strength of nationalism itself is a variable in determining the degree to which intramural differences significantly affect a nation's response to events outside the country. Conversely, sometimes a particular international issue will trigger or exacerbate internal antagonisms or rivalries, and will thus be decided more on the basis of conflicting internal interests than on any agreed national interest.

The question of relative homogeneity in domestic ethnic outlooks can be important even in long-established societies, such as in Northern Ireland, where the Irish-Catholic heroine Bernadette Devlin brought the differences between Protestants and Catholics in Londonderry to the debates of the United Nations (1970); or in Canada, where the late Charles de Gaulle upset international decorum by playing too much to the French-Canadian gallery while on an official visit to that country. The problem is much greater in a country like Malaysia, where Chinese and Malaysian ethnic groups maintain separate and very different identities; or Iraq, which Carlton Coon called a "mosaic" society, as Baghdad alone presented such separate ethnic identities as Muslim Arabs, Christian Arabs, Assyrians, Kurds, Jews, Turks, Persians, and Armenians.[5] Jordan is another example; its foreign policy vis-à-vis Israel is a daily contest between the more militant Palestinian refugees in Jordan, whose attitudes are dominated by a feeling of being dispossessed, and the Jordanians, who apparently see their own best interest in a less belligerent stance. European history of the last century cannot be understood without considering the role and sense of identity of ethnic minorities in the shifting boundaries of nation states. Trade and economic life in a whole series of countries in the Far East cannot be understood without considering the unique inclination toward industriousness, thrift, and ingenuity of the overseas Chinese minorities in these countries.

Considerations of ethnic diversity have been the daily fare of diplomats and of their foreign offices throughout history. However, the importance of this factor is not always appreciated by the novice in international operations, who is often too ready to undertake a foreign assignment without taking time for his homework. The background history and social description of an area are normally available in area study programs, which provide insight into the social and cultural basis for a country's contesting voices. Far too often priority is given to a practical but misguided preoccupation with getting to an assignment to fill an urgent vacancy on the assumption that one can learn about the country after arrival. This practice can lead to a bumbling performance born of innocent insensitivity to local rivalries and intergroup antagonisms.

Often the diplomat must try to comprehend not one national character, but several within a nation, if he is to make a realistic estimate of the public psychological pressures which can impinge on governmental decision-making processes. The process is compounded when one must anticipate when members of ethnic minorities will perceive and reason about international issues as members of their ethnic group and when as nationals. This question continually occurs in working with the Montagnards in Viet Nam, for example. When are they reacting as Montagnards, and when as Vietnamese?

Differing Degrees of Identification with International Issues

In terms of international affairs not all groups or segments of a national society are of equal importance. Some are more politically conscious and articulate than others; some are more deeply concerned with international issues than others. Logically the foreign affairs observer is most interested in the outlooks and patterns of reasoning which characterize those groups most likely to have an effect on a government's foreign policy. Other groups receive less attention even though they may be large, perhaps constituting a majority of the population. The observer does, however, need to be alert for changes, or for particular issues which will attract the interest of otherwise inert groups.

Even in well-informed and highly developed countries, individual awareness of and interest in the substantive elements of foreign affairs are often limited to a small part of the public.

As late as the mid-1960s, public opinion studies indicated that as much as one-fourth of the American population did not even know that a war was going on in Vietnam, much less have any appreciation of the role the United States was playing there. Even Americans in academic circles, who would normally be well informed in foreign affairs issues, had a dearth of knowledge about Viet Nam, and about the social and political system which existed there. They knew little about the issues which set the stage for the conflict, in which diverse South Vietnamese political and interest groups played a part along with North Viet Nam, the United States, and allied nations. Consequently, American government administrators were largely left to their own devices to conceptualize the issues according to their view of American interests. It included a keen awareness of the complex of American commitments in the international arena, anticipated negative consequences of the Viet Cong's going unopposed, military logistics problems, and such intelligence estimates as could be prepared on the basis of rather limited American official knowledge about the Indochina scene. Decisions were made on the basis of more or less conventional American foreign affairs wisdom and experience and intuitive assumptions as to what the American public would desire or consider in the American interest. Consequently, early decisions were made without much knowledge of the issues on the part of the American public, strong public feelings or attitudes, or any great sense of personal participation in choosing the course of action. Among the professionals in foreign affairs not working directly on Viet Nam matters, there was a frequent admission of uncertainty as to the wisdom of the many decisions along the way which added up to a heavy involvement. But with the uncertainty went a feeling that, in their limited understanding of Viet Nam, they did not know of any better course of action, and that they therefore would have to trust, tentatively at least, the conclusions of those closer to the action. What participatory interest the American public displayed in United States foreign affairs went to events and issues which were more in tune with American perceptions and existing cognitive worlds, i.e., European affairs, the cold war, arms, the space race. Psychologically, Viet Nam developments were distant, known only in fragments out of context, and too foreign to be easily integrated into the existing cognitive structures of most Americans.

By 1970 public awareness had changed markedly. Americans in the mass were not much more profoundly informed than before about the issues in the unfolding war, but they showed far more participatory concern and anxiety. The cumulative effect of news media, especially on-the-scene television coverage; the increasing numbers of friends and relatives directly involved; the shocking reports of the My Lai incident; and frustration with problems much closer to daily experience, which became associated, logically or otherwise, with the American role in the Indochina conflict, dramatically altered the American public's perception of the war.

The result was an equally dramatic change in domestic conditions for government decision making. In fact, this upheaval of public opinion is one of the more salient instances demonstrating that public diplomacy is the new reality in international affairs. Certainly the fact that the United States is one of the world's most participative democracies, endowed with the most highly developed technology in communication, set the stage for public diplomacy repercussions on a grand scale.

What happened in the U.S. suggests the kind of analysis often required to estimate the significance of various elements in a society when the potential impact of public opinion is to be determined. First, and most basically, to what degree does a segment of a population feel itself a part of a broader social or political universe, and thus identify with international issues at all? Secondly, to what extent are the typical psychological worlds of a national population or of groups within it tuned in to a given foreign affairs issue? The American public is relatively well informed, perhaps the best informed in the world. The American is relatively interested in people and events far from his immediate locale. He feels some common interest with all other Americans, and even with still larger portions of mankind. In other words, his "social universe" is large, at least when compared with those of many of the world's inhabitants. Yet when American involvement began in Viet Nam, the typical American cognitive world hardly included Viet Nam at all. There was little reason for perceptions to register or for strong opinions to surface. Until enough new knowledge and more reason for individual identification with events in Viet Nam were incorporated into the average American's thoughts and interests, there was little articulate reaction to U.S. policy decisions. The early policy, for better or for worse, was developed in something of a vacuum of general public opinion, as has happened before in American history—policy toward Latin America in the nineteenth and part of the twentieth century comes to mind. But after the communications media finally attracted American attention to Viet Nam, and especially after Viet Nam became associated in American cognitive processes with other existing anxieties and emotionally-laden issues closer to home, the effect of public attitudes on policy formation was strikingly different.

One would expect, then, that in nations, or in groups within nations, where the felt social universe is smaller and where concern and information about the outside world are more limited, the potential pressure of public opinion on international policy decisions would be less. The problem in all these cases is, however, that bits of new information can be absorbed without a basis for perspective, and can be mixed with existing cognitive components to form strange new mixtures. Thus the mass of Pakistanis and Indians who have no concern for the United States in their daily lives are acutely conscious of every item of new armament which the U.S. furnishes to the others' country. And in this climate, the writer of a letter to the editor of a

Karachi newspaper claimed that Americans listening to the Muhammad Ali-Joe Frazier boxing match in 1971 gloated over Ali's defeat because he was a Moslem.

All of this is relevant to the utility of public opinion polling. One must remember, however, that even if the polling technology is professional and well-adapted to the local culture, some rather fundamental questions about the practical importance of the various segments of opinion have to be answered before results can be interpreted.

Social Stratification and New Middle Classes

Now let us look more specifically at the sociologist's concept "social stratification" as a factor in social and political perceptions and judgments. The idea of social stratification is familiar. Anthropologist W. Lloyd Warner's Yankee City studies [6] have been reported widely enough so that such terms as "upper-middle" or "lower-upper" class have entered popular speech, and in any case, the words "upper crust" or "working class" are common parlance. What is not so familiar, particularly to an American, is the extent to which perception can be preconditioned by a consciousness of stratification. The American's all-pervading middle-class orientation tends to blind him to the full effect of class division, for it provides him with a unique lens through which to view the world. If we recognize that a person's "world view" is affected by his position in relation to other people, it is apparent that where one fits into the social structure has much to do with one's typical social perceptions. Much of the humor of the comic strip "Beetle Bailey" is a play on the differing outlooks from the various ranks in a military social structure, as was the humor in the famous Bill Mauldin cartoons of World War II.

"Social class" refers, of course, to the hierarchical division of a society in terms of social prestige, authority, privilege, affluence, occupation, or other criteria significant in that society. "Class" is an abstraction; it is observed only through a composite of behavior patterns which permit some definition of social divisions. "Class" implies some social mobility, whereas "caste" implies a more rigidly ascribed status, which is not subject to change within a society, and is determined by birth. Though class is sometimes hard to define with the accuracy a practical man would like, such stratification is real, and it has a great effect on the way in which people relate themselves to each other and form their concept of self, their aspirations, their hierarchy of values, and their total social viewpoint.

It was suggested above that the way labor groups see themselves and their role in their society is, in part, a function of differing class structures in their respective societies. That is, labor's perspective on such matters as labor-management relations or economic and political issues is closely related to underlying basic assumptions, concerns, and habitual ways of thinking which are tied to their class or caste position within their society. It was also pointed out in Chapter II that many of the American's typical preconceptions in approaching foreign policy problems are logical extensions of his assumptions based on values found in the achievement-oriented, individualistic, egalitarian mainstream of America's middle-class society. It is apparent that decision makers in nations which lack the degree of middle-class orientation characteristic of the United States (and most nations differ in some degree in this respect) will be subject to very different kinds of public pressure.

The foreign affairs arena in which the social structure-perception relationship assumes its most obvious importance is in the ideological struggle between the Communist and the Western democratic persuasions, for the contrast between the two lies precisely in the completely different conception of social structure. The Communist viewpoint, with its inspiration in the writings of Karl Marx, started with a preoccupation with the relationship between traditional, rigidly structured society on the one hand, and economic structure, the structure of government, and the well-being of the mass of the population on the other. The orthodox Communist theory of society considers economic factors to be the driving force of all social and political relationships (and behavioral science is understandably suspicious of single-factor explanations).

Even though the Communists get themselves into theoretical traps by this unbalanced stress on economic factors as the prime motivation of social life, their assumption that stratified society is the central issue in social change and even in revolution is a key element in understanding their communication with societies in which a large part of the people also carry as a "given" in their cognitive organization the view that the established society is stratified, and not in their favor. It is simply the product of their life experience, one they have been aware of from an early age. They do not need to think about it. It "makes sense" to see social issues as functions of social stratification. Thus, when the Communist tries to communicate with this part of the world, he starts with a similarity in basic assumptions. This fact is highly important in understanding the appeals of Communism.

In turn, the American tradition of individualism, and of an open-class, achievement-oriented society really makes sense only to people who have experienced it. That experience is relatively limited to the United States and to a few similar societies such as Canada and Australia, but even in those countries there are subtle differences. People in much of the world see the American ideology as an abstraction. It is often an ideal concept, and thus a powerful ideological force around the world—but an abstraction none the less. When thus perceived, even if the idea is attractive, the American ideology is more subject to debate, to examination, to intellectual testing in the minds of those who have not shared the American experience as the "natural" organization of social life. Without the experience of living with it, it is harder to take cognizance of the basic yet routine elements of American thought and value patterns which go along with the actual everyday operation of the American ideology. Hence the misconception of our "materialism," as was mentioned in Chapter II. Also, it is easier for the outsider not steeped in American experience to perceive—accurately or not—the discrepancies or contradictions between ideology and practice.

It is easy to overstate the contrast, perhaps. The United States is not without some class, and even near-caste, distinctions, and few older societies still retain intact completely rigid patterns of social stratification. The contrast may be only relative in some cases, yet the difference is reflected in differing national modes of personality organization. Therefore, differing perception patterns associated with differing social organizations constitute a very real aspect of the international ideological contest. Contrasting views of social structure help explain why the short-lived U.S. attempt to explain itself as "people's capitalism" was such a failure. It was an attempt to convince the foreign audience that American capitalism does not correspond to the old image of overbearing exploitation of the masses by a few at the top, but that it is a system in which everyone has a share in the ownership and in the fruits of production. Exhibits provided graphic explanations of how production facilities are owned by public participation in stocks and showed the household gadgets which the "people" shared. But the cognitive organization of an audience not tuned to the idea that workers could be private stockholders did not permit an easy acceptance of "people's capitalism" in the way intended. It was perceived as an absurdity, as a contradiction of terms, and as a misrepresentation.

Perhaps the most interesting studies in perception and class position concern areas where new middle-class groups are now in the formation process. Their view of the world and their vested interest in international issues are becoming highly significant. These groups are nationalistic in sentiment and are rapidly assuming positions of power in their societies. The new middle sectors are developing in the traditional societies as the positions which go along with a more modern society are being filled. Skilled labor, white-collar workers, bureaucrats, school teachers, salesmen, professional men, and university students are on the increase, sometimes beyond their society's capacity to absorb them. In many cases these groups occupy the place of what corresponds to the middle class in the Western world, but they are still "sectors" or "middle segments" because their life styles, habits, and self-images have not yet crystalized into an integrated subculture which might be called a middle class. Yet their beliefs and anxieties, values and motivations are among the most important forces pressing on new governments, and consequently on these governments' strategies and policies in the international arena. It is worth while to look more closely at the sociopsychological task facing these new middle sectors.

Their psychological adaptation problem can be appreciated more readily by tracing the development of their new status. Let us consider a simplified or "ideal" case—a traditional two-class society with a small elite or aristocratic group at the top and a peasantry at the bottom. Imagine the social class range with the middle level left out, in other words, a society with no provision for a middle class. This picture is obviously oversimplified for most times and places, yet it has an essential correctness for many societies in the past and for some traditional societies which survive to the present with little real social change. Much of Latin America would have fit this design only a generation ago.

In such a model, prestige comes automatically for those in the small elite at the top; they are born into the upper social strata. The attributes of wealth, education, property, and influence come naturally and as a matter of social expectation. Travel is theirs if they wish it; practice and enjoyment of the arts and literature is their prerogative. They do not need to validate their status or worry about losing it, for it is ascribed by virtue of who they are, not by what they have made of themselves.

For most of the people in the lower echelons their position is humble—part of the mass base. Traditional peasants are poor, uneducated, tied to the land and often to some member of the elite as a serf or a near slave, although in many places such a peasantry has held an independent existence. The peasant's position also comes with birth, and his normal expectations and outlook on life have to conform to the reality of a peasant's unchanging social status. Thus he is normally well-adjusted if he is fatalistic in outlook, resigned, and aware that his lot will be difficult and that his fate, for better or worse, will be determined by higher forces—human or supernatural—and is beyond his power of direct intervention. Such peasants may be aware of the affluence and privilege of the upper groups, but they do not identify with it or necessarily resent it. The possibility of the traditional peasant rising to the elite is too distant to be thinkable. Perhaps he could believe in an eventual utopia, or a happy afterlife, but for the present he can do little beyond petition the forces which he thinks do control his fortune—the landlord, the governor, the deity. To think of personal achievement or getting ahead by hard work and ingenuity would be a poor adjustment to real-life conditions, and the peasant society does not teach its sons to think that way. A documented picture of such a part of society, now changing, is provided in Daniel Lerner's *The Passing of Traditional Society.*[7]

In such social stratification interaction between the two groups is not necessarily lacking. It can be close and sustained. But the social meaning of the interaction and the status identification is always clear. The elite remain the elite. They forthrightly expect deference and service from their social inferiors. They may also expect to assume some paternal responsibility for the guidance and well-being of the lower-status group within their sphere of influence, as on an estate. The culture normally establishes certain codes of decency and restraint for the elite, which are recognized by all, and also customs of respect and service to be practiced by the peasantry—again recognized by all. The peasant thinks like a peasant, has peasant likes and dislikes, peasant fears and anxieties. He has a peasant self-image, and he perceives the world about him in peasant terms.

This model is set up for analytical purposes. In the modern world social relationships have changed greatly, and few societies remain in which it would be found in its pure form. Yet vestiges of this kind of social stratification do exist, and the thinking which goes with it persists even in many parts of modern Europe and in parts of the United States where some degree of peasant, e.g., slave, society existed. In much of the developing world the basic social assumptions which derive from such social history persist in agricultural and landholding systems, in industrial management relations, in government bureaucracy, and in social relations in general.

On the other side of the picture, I have encountered a surviving example of the elite self-image. A few years ago I conducted a training session for a group of American government personnel who had recently arrived at a large overseas post. The subject of the seminar was the significance of contrasting social stratification in communicating in the local area. When the group was asked to what social class they belonged, there was general agreement: middle class. To add a note of humor, I asked if anyone there belonged to the upper class. The group laughed, but one woman did raise her hand. More laughter. However, the lady was serious; she lowered her hand in some embarrassment and confusion. As it turned out, she was the European wife of an American officer, and in her country she *was* upper class. But she had not learned that in American public gatherings one does not say so. Such social assumptions are normal in more highly stratified societies, but are rejected as presumptuous in popular American thinking.

Even in today's surviving traditional societies, the two-strata system does *not* exist in such a simple form. People *do* occupy an in-between status, perhaps as few as 5% of the population in some less developed nations, or 25% to 30% in others. Some members of the new middle sectors come from the old elite, but most of them come from below, as the boundary delineating the old peasant society fades. They come from the lower strata not only because of the new occupations and the higher incomes but also—and this is most important—for psychological reasons. The expanded social horizon which comes to them with modern communication brings a rejection of their peasant status and an identification with the new mobility. In fact, identification with middle-sector status has come more rapidly than middle-sector income or job opportunities. A rural school teacher in many parts of the world would be solidly middle-sector, psychologically, for example, yet earn wages allowing little more than a subsistence-level standard of living. People with undiluted peasant backgrounds move to the urban slums in response to the stirrings of their self-images and their rising expectations, hoping to enter into the lower reaches of industrial labor or other modern employment, and adding further pressure to the revolution of rising expectations.

Consequently, many people in rapidly changing societies now occupy the ground of middle-class society in societies which had *never provided for a middle-class culture.* Not accepted into the old elite, and certain that they are peasants no longer, these new middle groups lack the all-important definition of who they are in the society. They have neither a set of integrated customs and social habits for middle-class living, nor a supporting set of concepts to define their self-esteem as middle-class citizens. They have moved into a vacuum in terms of culture and personality, and what the outsider is observing is a psychological struggle in which they are adapting, innovating, and trying to integrate the new values and thought patterns which will serve them in societies which had never before included any sizable middle class. These patterns will have to become institutionalized into their own minds and into the minds of the rest of the society, eventually establishing a middle-class culture, and providing for its practitioners some sense of security, identity, and purpose. In urban Mexico, where the new middle groups are in their second and third generation, this transition is well under way.

The difference in psychological circumstance between the

long-established culture of the West, which supports its middle classes, and the search-for-a-culture qualities of the middle sectors of societies in more rapid transition explains some of the difficulties in international communication between one middle-class group and another, and also suggests some explanation of what is going on in ideological ferment. These new sectors are articulate, and often powerful out of proportion to their size. They often include the political leaders and the communicators— members of the press and radio services, school teachers, artists and writers, professional military, and the government bureaucracy.[8] They are becoming the new elite. On the one hand, American middle-class society presents an attractive ideological influence, with its respect for the individual achiever and its precedent for mass democratic participation in local and national government processes. On the other, these new groups are in a hurry. By the very nature of their position they are seeking to revolutionize social structure. The revolutionary movements of recent history appeal to them, especially if they are frustrated in their attempts to achieve their new expectations by the limitations of existing economic and social systems or by limitations imposed on their democratic participation in still-transitional societies.

Overseas Americans tend to believe that it is easier to communicate with this group than it actually is. On the surface they appear to be a middle-class counterpart whose style parallels middle-class life in the United States in many respects. Often they are host nationals who have considerable experience in working with Americans, who have learned a behavior which bridges the gap for the purposes of carrying out international business or technical assistance programs. Yet in their total personal life there are many inconsistencies. Old ways persist; status remains ill-defined. Sometimes they are more American than the Americans; sometimes they display value symbols borrowed from the traditional elites, such as avoiding working with their hands, or placing inordinate emphasis on degrees and titles. (It has been reported from South Asia that among other full-blown uses of academic titles, the item "Cambridge Examination (failed)" has been noted. Apparently in an area where education is a mark of prestige, it is important to let the public know that one was qualified to *take* the Cambridge Examination, even though, unfortunately, one failed it.)

At the least it is different to be a member of a middle-class minority rather than of a middle-class majority; these new middle sectors face more frustrations in such matters as obtaining middle-class levels of income, and in knowing where they are accepted socially. This group is often concerned with problems of national identity, and in the process becomes particularly touchy and critical in communication with foreigners from better-developed countries for which their feelings may be ambivalent. Thus, even pro-Western new nationalists sometimes derive a certain amount of satisfaction in seeing a major power taken down a little by a smaller one—from being defeated in tennis matches to having their fishing boats arrested for ignoring a smaller country's self-declared extensive off-shore territorial claim.

The impact and consequences of social change have given rise to an extensive literature and much attention in academic forums, in policy statements, and in the debates of the United Nations. Terms such as "the revolution of rising expectations," "new elites," and the "north-south confrontation" pay tribute to deep and meaningful changes in much of the world. The consequence of this social change for foreign policy processes derives from the ever increasing part played by the new middle sectors in many nations, and from the patterns of perception which characterize them. They may appear inconsistent or irrational in the pressures which they bring to bear on their governments, but their attitudes and concerns can assume an overriding importance to their governments when domestic issues are considered; and governments often must speak to this segment when foreign affairs are concerned.

Social Structure and Perception—Role Analysis

Sir Winston Churchill's account of the events surrounding the fall of France in World War II and the subsequent British decision to destroy part of the French fleet in Oran recalls the part played by Admiral Darlan. Darlan commanded the French fleet up to the time of the French cabinet crisis in 1940, which led to French capitulation to Germany without providing for formal governmental liaison in exile with Great Britain. Over the years he had directed the development of the fleet, making it a highly efficient naval organization—at that time France was the fourth naval power in the world. His devotion was to the fleet; he had promised that it would never fall into German hands. As France fell, and even up to the morning following the fall of Reynaud's cabinet, he declared his intention to French General Georges to order the fleet to sail for British, American, or French colonial harbors rather than fall as prizes of war to the Germans. His command would have been obeyed, but Darlan was named Minister of Marine in the Laval cabinet, and the order was not given. The next day when General Georges asked Darlan what had happened to make him change his mind, he answered simply "I am now Minister of Marine." [9] His new duty was a political responsibility rather than one of naval command, and that duty, as he saw it, was to keep the fleet intact with the government of France—of which he was Minister of Marine—whatever the fate of France. In reversing himself in one of history's most significant command decisions, Darlan apparently did not receive any new information to make him change his mind: *His concept of his role had changed as his status changed.*

There remains, then, in our discussion of social structure, the *status and role* concept. A person's perception and response depend in large part on who he thinks he is. His self-image helps select which aspects of a situation are meaningful, and influences his concept of what action is appropriate. As man is a social animal, this self-image and concept of correct role is defined in part by the group's consensus on what roles, that is, expected behavior, go with the various status positions recognized by the group. "Status positions" do not necessarily mean positions of prestige. They range from such everyday and almost universal positions as father, son, or trader through such special occupations as bartender or schoolteacher, to more exclusive positions like Minister of Foreign Affairs or Chief of State. Less specific status positions include friend, teammate, client, fellow commuter.

Communication also is closely related to status and role. What one chooses to say, what one chooses to hear, and how one chooses to respond are functions of mental images of social identity—who one is—in the communication situation, and what one's rights, duties, and obligations are in the communication relationship. Analyzing these perception factors is somewhat less abstract than relating perception to ethnic divisions and class distinctions, as role analysis can be directed more specifically to definable individuals and to more specific categories of people. In foreign affairs and public diplomacy, role concept is more directly applicable to person-to-person communication, including diplomatic negotiation, than to estimating the perception and response of large segments of a population. Status and role are the basis of social relationships, and as such are among the sociologist's most fundamental concerns in developing theories and concepts of social structure.

Before proceeding further with the interrelationships between culture, role, and perception, it might be helpful to note how, from a psychological point of view, a person's "reference group" influences his choice of behavior. Man's cognitive machinery—his human "computer" — is normally "programmed" to store in its "memory bank" an awareness of certain people whose judgments, approval, or censure are important to him. As the brain-computer scans its circuits in processing a perception and a response, the anticipated value judgments of these other people are included as a relevant factor, sometimes consciously, sometimes not. These meaningful people may include his family, close friends, colleagues, members of his graduating class; in some instances, even strangers in the street. In social psychology and sociology they have been defined as the "reference group."

One key to understanding an individual's behavior is knowing who, specifically, make up his "reference group" in a particular situation. Whose judgments and opinions does he take into account, consciously or otherwise, when he chooses a course of action, evaluates the morality of what he does, or takes stock of his personal worth and success? And how important a part do these reference personalities play in the decision at hand? Even in a technical matter, let us say, of deciding whether to issue a visa, a vice-consul may have in the back of his mind the hoped-for approval of his superior, the consul, the knowledge that some of his friends think all travel should be unrestricted, the fear that the applicant will think him overbearing and needlessly technical if he refuses, and perhaps an awareness of his wife's prejudice against the class of immigrant before him. All these subtle aspects might bear to some degree on his decision. Other examples could be found, *ad infinitum*. Thus "reference group" is another concept which can aid in comprehending the social dimension of perception and response, and it can be applied to people, including officials, in all societies. It ties in well with role concept, to which we now return.

Social roles are learned patterns of behavior, learned from the society and shared with other members of the society. That is, roles are part of culture, or, turned around, culture steps in to say what kind of behavior is expected to go with the group's various status positions. Role playing is an important function in any society, for it makes behavior more predictable—an essential to social life. To use everyday examples, one generally knows ahead of time when he goes into a business office how one is expected to relate to the receptionist, secretary, clerk, or janitor. Role expectations may go beyond the actual technical demands of the situation. A ranking university professor might be expected to smoke a pipe rather than a cigar; a banker wears conservative clothes; a school teacher must be more circumspect in personal life than an actor. More basically, a father is expected to provide for his family; the wife does the cooking and the laundry (a role now contested by the Women's Liberation movement); children obey their teachers; adults are not supposed to enjoy children's games or act like children; and women are not supposed to talk like men. All may not play their roles as they are supposed to, but most do, and this reduces the confusion in social relations.

Hence "role" is a concept that is similar in technical and in popular use, except for extending the implications. Each culture and society defines roles and depends on them to give consistency to human behavior, to provide for division of labor and cooperation, and to provide patterns of behavior which are predictable and dependable. The sociology teacher often illustrates the role concept by going back to Shakespeare's *As You Like It:* "All the world's a stage, and all the men and women merely players. They have their exits and their entrances, and one man in his time plays many parts." Then Shakespeare takes his imaginary player through the various roles he plays in his progression from infancy to old age. The old man is not expected to think or talk or act like a youth—there is an appropriate way for him to behave, which befits his dignity and age. Role is more complicated for the sociologist than for Shakespeare, perhaps, because in any complex society one necessarily plays many roles during the course of a single day: husband, father, office chief, member of a working group, drinking companion, or whatever. Sometimes roles conflict, adding to the pressures of complex society.

We noted above that people do not always play their roles in all their customary details. The deacon may drive a red sports car; the pediatrician may chew gum and hang around pool halls; the banker may have a mistress (which might be quite acceptable in some cultures). The important point is that society works more smoothly when both the incumbent of a status position and his social group share an image of what kind of rights, duties, obligations, and modes of reaction go with their assigned roles. There is a pattern; and when the pattern is broken, it is a deviation from a norm which may or may not be serious enough to demand some kind of sanction. But at least there is a pattern, and behavior is not capricious. The inability to predict what is going to happen is a source of anxiety; culture's function is to relieve anxiety, just as it provides patterns to secure food or to raise children.

When interaction and communication are cross-cultural, problems can appear if status and role are defined differently in the different cultures. Some status positions may exist in one culture, and not in another. Americans have no clearly defined roles for camel drivers, Buddhist priests, ceremonial relatives, or for the arrangers and go-betweens found in the Far East. Thus the American does not know just how to interact with a camel driver or a Buddhist monk except perhaps to photograph him. Conversely, many cultures have no clearly defined roles for management consultants, fashion models, or statisticians. In all these cases communication is stilted until somehow a basis is established to fill in an image and get an answer to the questions "To whom am I speaking?" "How can I expect him to behave?"

Frequently in intercultural communication, similar, or apparently similar, status positions exist in each culture, but the roles are defined differently. Or *formal* status positions equate in role to the extent that job descriptions (as in a government bureaucracy) or technical demands are alike. But the more subtle or informal role expectations may differ as the cultural context and social structure in which the roles are embedded differ. A policeman may have similar job descriptions in England and in India, as it was the British who established police forces in India, but no one in India expects an Indian policeman to behave just like a London bobby. Subtle interrelated aspects such as educational level, class or caste distinctions, ideas about government employees, or about law enforcement and justice have their impact on role behavior. The two societies may differ greatly in their concepts of what constitutes a "good" police force, or of what behavior should be considered illegal. This seems obvious enough. Yet without thinking, the Englishman in India will tend to judge the Indian policeman on the basis of role expectations for British policemen; the European traveling in the United States judges the taxi driver or the waitress on the basis of an image he holds for those who render similar services at home.

The concept of contrasting role analysis is so important in person-to-person communication in international affairs that the point may be belabored a bit. In a sample practical application, let us say that an American official has occasion to negotiate at length with the Minister of Public Works in a country in which traditional government institutions are in the process of being modernized. The following questions might serve as a guide to understanding how that minister of public works sees his own role, and how his society defines his role in both its formal and informal details:

How does one get to be Minister of Public Works in this country? What qualifications make one a candidate for the position? Must one be a competent engineer, an administrator? Is it important and does it add to one's authority to have high *social* competence by being a member of a good family, by being cultured and educated, or by being upper-class? Must one be a supporter of the political party in power or a representative of a particular political supporting group, or of an ethnic or religious group? Should one have traveled abroad, and hold a degree from a foreign university? Should one be old or young? Must one be a personal friend and confidant, or even a relative of the president or the prime minister?

Of all the qualifying characteristics which might be important, which of these items stand out as most important to cabinet ministers themselves? Recognition of which quality is most pleasing to the incumbent?

Technically, what is the Minister of Public Works supposed to do? What kind of office does he direct? How much authority does he have? How does the structure of his government define his position? Who else shares authority in public works? What is the history of public works in his country? What performance does the public expect?

Informally, what is the Minister of Public Works supposed to do? Should he get public works constructed as efficiently as possible, or provide jobs for needy people? How is the Minister supposed to manage public works funds—account for them strictly, or use them to accomplish certain political objectives? Is he supposed to pay full attention to the job, or play politics either for himself or for the prime minister? Is he essentially a figurehead with technical experts in his department actually tending to public works, or is he really in charge? Or is the prime minister really in charge and responsible for the final decision?

What symbols of status go with the job, and which are important? Is there an official car and driver? Aides, a photographer, and an entourage of assistants? An office near the prime minister? Direct access to the public, or much formality and protocol in the office? Is public deference expected toward a cabinet minister? Is it more prestigious to be Minister of Public Works, or of Education or Foreign Affairs—how does he rank with other cabinet ministers? What are the forms and customs of address, of introduction, or of reference to the Minister in print?

What elements go into the social "image" of cabinet ministers? Must he live well with a fine house, servants, and expensive dress? Must he live on his salary, or is there an informal expectation that a cabinet minister is already wealthy or will become wealthy in office? Is a minister carefully sober and circumspect in his personal life, or does his status permit, or even give license to, behavior which would not be considered proper by people of lower station? Must he honor religious practice? Must he give graduation speeches? Should he exude authority, or be democratic in his dealing with the public? Should he pose as an authority only on public works, or because he is a cabinet minister, is he expected to be an authority on everything? Finally—specifically, who is the incumbent, and how well does he play the standard role? What are his personal characteristics? When is he playing the role of his office, and when is he himself? When will he react as Minister of Public Works, and when as himself?

Undoubtedly many more questions could be asked which would help fill out the picture of the minister's role, or even of conflicting roles expected of him by different parts of his public. Even if the minister is able to step out of his role when working with foreign officials, he must play his role in his own society, and his decisions must be somewhat consistent with it, even in situations of rapid social change and innovation.[10]

In diplomacy and in countless intergovernmental working-level situations there is a constant need to judge authority and decision-making power, to understand a foreign public's reactions to its leaders, to predict how self-images of role will affect decisions. The importance of careful role analysis can hardly be overstated, whether it is done in sociological terms or by other conceptual approaches. Not the least of our problems in international activities is assuring that our foreign colleagues and foreign government policy makers understand American role behavior. How can a foreign official know, for example, which speech of which official is the official policy? How can he judge the authority an official has if he is criticized in the press or is the subject of unflattering cartoons? How does he know, when an American official adheres strictly to a regulation, whether he has no other choice or whether he just does not wish to be helpful? How does he know that the man who is everybody's friend, wears loud sport shirts in public, and drives his own station wagon is really the chargé d'affaires? (In reverse, on far too many occasions ranking officials in South Asia have been received by Americans with considerably less dignity than their status merited simply because they "were dressed in old pajamas.")

Role analysis has a further application when governmental institutions change, either in the process of planned development programs or as a result of social upheavals such as war or revolution. New institutions, especially as they are being modernized, require new roles. It is difficult to establish such new roles, for it is not only a matter of a new incumbent learning them but of his society learning them too as a matter of their expectations and ideas about their officials and public servants.

A skilled and respected British teacher, who stayed on in Malaya after independence, was asked by the new government to conduct seminars for the Malayan civil service, which was formerly under British supervision. The object specifically was to introduce a new concept of role: The civil servant was to be judged no longer by how well he served a British bureaucracy, but by how well he served his own newly-independent public. His authority and prestige no longer reflected the British administration, but depended on the definitions of his own society. The more one considers the nuances involved in this transition, the more one must appreciate the problem posed for the seminar. Somehow the civil servant had to change his reference group, his self-image, his view of his own authority, his manner of working with his colleagues and with his public, and even his style of life outside the office.

Role expectations complicate international communication at many other points, in both official and nonofficial intercourse. The role of "citizen" may not equate with "citizen" in another society and culture. Nor perhaps does "worker," "professor," "partner," or "university student."

One of the more entertaining—and at the same time instructive—treatises on contrasts in role behavior is John Patrick's play *Teahouse of the August Moon.* In it American occupation forces try to establish democracy in Okinawa, but the American officers finally capitulate in their attempts to establish such roles as mayor, teacher, treasurer, and ladies of the League for Democratic Action. Finally the Americans adopt Okinawan dress and outlook and enjoy the teahouse and the geisha entertainment, which miraculously materializes instead of a pentagon-shaped schoolhouse.

Most to the point is the American's task in evaluating the potential for democratic leadership or popular participation in government in areas in which the United States has some kind of concern. Viet Nam, Latin America, or the Weimar Republic of a few years ago are examples. How well democratic institutions can be exported depends not only on their acceptance as formal structures but also on the acceptance of new roles. The latter is more difficult. A formal government institution can be written into a constitution, but role behavior is a matter of culture and shared habits in thinking and expectations. It is difficult to explain roles; it is even harder to transfer them from one society to another.[11]

I V

How Preconceptions

about Institutions Affect

International Communication

ALMOST A HALF-CENTURY AGO, DURING THE EARLY stages of a career which was to have a profound influence on American thinking about world affairs, Walter Lippmann wrote a book entitled *Public Opinion*.[1] In introducing the psychological imponderables implicit in his subject, he used the highly descriptive phrase "pictures in our heads." It has been popular in communications circles ever since. Lippmann used it to contrast the world as it appeared to the individual with the actual "world outside," to remind his readers that people's responses to events, large and small, are conditioned by preconceptions of that world, by existing mental "pictures" which fill in detail and meaning not necessarily supplied by the real event. (In fact, Lippmann explained the problem of perception in foreign affairs very well, and without the aid of behavioral science!) His apt terminology can be extended to present problems of communication, and to the part which preconceptions play in international dialogues.

The question in any meaningful communication is whether the preconceptions or "pictures in our heads" accurately reflect the situation or coincide with those of the person with whom we are communicating. In cross-cultural communication the chances are higher that they do not. And the more abstract the subject the more difficult it is to test a preconception with direct evidence or to be sure how well it corresponds with the image held by the other party. Consequently, mismatched preconceptions become a greater problem as the level of abstraction of ideas rises; the mismatch may not be recognized at all, and in any case will be hard to manage. In this chapter we will concentrate on *institutions*, the idea level at which much serious international communication takes place, and the level at which we are hard pressed to assure accurate communication and interpretation.

Institutions as Subjects of International Communication

Much of the time in foreign affairs analysis and discussion we are concerned with some kind of institution: governmental, political, social, or economic. Any formal diplomatic relationship involves governments and the foreign offices within them—which are institutionalized entities. The substance of diplomacy typically involves such institutions as political parties, industries, financial organizations, the press, universities, or exporting and importing businesses. In multilateral diplomacy one is confronted with dozens of international organizations which have become enduring institutions. Technical assistance is concerned with modernizing "institutions" in developing countries.

All the parties involved in communicating about such institutions do so with a supporting composite of ideas about them which go well beyond the technical facts that can be readily described or written into organization manuals. If single words can differ in connotation according to the differing experiences of those who use or hear them, it is obvious that the full meaning or "picture" of the still more abstract "institution" will differ greatly when contrasting national experience and cultural environment are considered. Note the possibilities for varied subjective meaning around the world in this random sample of institutions: General Motors, the League of Women Voters, Pravda, the International Monetary Fund, the United States Navy, a police force, or even the family.

Institutions can be studied in many ways. Traditionally, in civics textbooks, governmental and many social and economic institutions have been described as formal structures with roots in law and regulation, with their own history and intended rationale. More recently, the emphasis has shifted to the *function* of institutions. A still different approach is that of the social psychologist, which studies institutions in terms of cognitive structures, that is, in terms of the assumptions, knowledge, attitudes, and expectations of the people concerned with the institution. It includes both those directly included in its structure (for example, in the case of a legislature, its presiding officers, members, assistants and clerks) and the larger society (the voters, taxpayers, those to be controlled by legislation). This approach locates institutions, in effect, in the mental processes of people, and emphasizes that the way they are perceived and understood is determined by the total experience with the institution in the culture.

Thus we deal with institutions in their psychological dimension. The tourist enjoys the foreign bazaar not simply because of the technical differences in the ways of buying and selling, but for its "atmosphere" as a social institution, with people relating to each other in new ways, buying and selling with differing tastes and for differing purposes. Both Frenchmen and visitors mourn the passing of Les Halles—the traditional market in the center of Paris—not because of economic considerations in its replacement but because of a complex of sentiments and subjective associations which made Les Halles the institution it was. The businessman abroad dealing with a foreign corporation faces a much larger task than understanding the production process or the management chart. He has to capture the local picture of business motivation, the customs in buying and selling, local appeals of the product, even how to reward the secretary at Christmas.

The cross-cultural communications task, then, is to anticipate the nature of the preconceptions one's counterpart is likely to have—to anticipate his image of the institutions under discussion. This objective merits a closer examination of institutions as a basic concept.

The Social Psychology of Institutions

Despite the fact that institutions are such a key subject in international affairs, the foreign affairs community tends to use the term loosely and imprecisely. In going to a foreign country, one recognizes that one should know something about that country's institutions, but then one rarely consults available sources to learn how specific institutional structures function or how these functions contrast with those in other nations and other cultures.

The sociologist's conception of an institution starts with the idea that within the total range of customs and social habits that make up the collective life of a society, institutions are more manageable subdivisions, or perhaps "packages" of customs, which pertain to some central objective or activity, and which involve coordinating the action of groups of people.

A good example is a business corporation. It combines in one package the customary practices in investment, management, work organization and technique, role expectations, accounting practices, and sense of purpose so that the combined activity of all the people involved produces a product or a service. A family is an institution in the same way; as one of its central functions conventional patterns of activity are assigned to its members and coordinated to the end that the children are protected, cared for, and educated until they can survive in the society.

Sociologists consider that institutions have, among other

attributes, a generally recognized purpose; a membership, and usually a clientele, with status positions and roles to go with them; usually some equipment or physical property; supporting beliefs and value systems which give sanction to what is done in the name of the institution; symbols and ceremonies; and provisions for continuity, such as rules and socialization techniques by which new members can be introduced into the institution's operation. Neither the observer nor the participant ever sees all the units of patterned behavior at one time, or all the structured relationships between people which together make an institution.

Thus, what makes institutions stick together is the mental programming on the part of all concerned—the complex of shared knowledge, assumptions, beliefs, and expectations regarding the function of the institution and the behavior of the people involved in it. In fact, institutionalized behavior is proof of the relationship between society and culture on the one hand, and personality on the other, for if the people did not think somewhat alike and rather automatically about a particular institution, the intricate coordination of behavior which must go with that institution would come to an end. Specific individuals may come and go, newcomers can learn their appropriate pattern of behavior, and the institution can go on. This sharing of cognitive factors gives an institution an elusive quality of existence above and beyond the sum of the activities of the specific individuals involved.

If the pattern of mental customs did not exist in the modal personality of the social group, each newcomer would face a new negotiating process as to how things should be done, who does what, for what reason—all the questions which the institution has already answered. Therefore, it is the psychological dimension of institutions which assures continuity, and makes them resistant to change, for to change an institution it is not enough to change the rules formally or technically. The change has to take place in the supporting mental customs which surround the institution.

Many institutions are supported by written laws, or by rules and regulations, which may be enforced by the government and even by international law. The temptation, then, is to use the legal description to explain an institution's operation, as this aspect is easier to see and deal with. But the routine operation of institutions does not rely on a daily reading of the rules; it depends on habitual thinking of participants and clients. Supporting beliefs and expectations about institutions which are basic and traditional, such as those relating to family, religion, traditional government, or land and agriculture, may be deeply held and emotionally laden. Sanction is strong, and supporting ideas are not subject to rapid change. Trying to change racially-segregated schools in parts of the United States where this practice has been institutionalized is a case in point. At a less personal level, as in the case of an industry or an international organization, the thought processes may not be as deeply ingrained, sanction less emotionally based, and change easier.

The idea that one part of an institution is the body of shared assumptions and expectations in the minds of its membership and clientele is especially important when new institutions are created. There tends to be a gap between the time that a formal institution is established, with its new rules and organizational chart, and the time that it is "institutionalized" in the minds of the people concerned. The United Nations, for example, has been created; its delegates meet according to its rules; it functions. But it is difficult for an institution to do more than its society, a world society in this case, expects it to do as a matter of course. Sociologically, the United Nations is still in the process of becoming institutionalized in its fuller meaning, of sinking roots into the assumptions and expectations of world society. Repeated successes speed up the process of its becoming part of the thinking habits of the politically conscious world.

Holding it at arm's length from key issues slows its full development, or allows it to become institutionalized at some intermediate level of involvement in international relationships.

This "basic assumptions" component of institutions also helps explain the difficulty in making large changes in the function of institutions. For instance, demands for preferential trade agreements which come from developing countries in the course of UNCTAD talks (United Nations Conference on Trade and Development) threaten all the assumptions of international trade institutions which are moving in the direction of freer trade through GATT (General Agreement on Tariffs and Trade). The assumptions of GATT are that it is good to have free trade and to allow the interaction of world price levels and the efficiency of producers to increase the total volume of goods and services available for everyone. In the argument for preferential market agreements, the assumptions are quite different, involving such matters as fairness and insuring greater income and development benefits for precisely those countries whose products do not compete well in world trade and whose production is not the most efficient. It would not be too difficult to change the rules of world trading institutions, but it would be a formidable task to turn around all the assumptions about trade which go with them, and which have developed in the industrialized part of the world over a period of many years.

The Comparative Approach

Let us turn now to further implications for cross-cultural communication. Considering how many elements make up an institution, especially in the psychological dimension, it is apparent that there is little chance that in all its nuances an institution in one country will be exactly like that of its counterpart in another, even though the formal structures are the same. (For example, insurance companies appear to be very similar, on paper, in Germany, Mexico, Italy, and the United States.)

Any institution operates in the context of all the other institutions and cultural patterns of its host society. The mental processes which go with institutions also must fit into the total configuration of cognitive elements which we have described as modal personality or national character. Thus any adequate comparative analysis of an institution requires some means of coming to grips with the way in which a sense of this interrelatedness contributes to the contrasting preconceptions held regarding that institution in differing societies, or adds detail to the contrasting "pictures" of that institution which may be carried in one's head.

The behavioral scientists do this by employing some form of structure-function analysis. That is, they analyze a given "structure"—an institution for the purposes of discussion here—in terms of the functions which it serves in the society as a whole, and the consequences it has for other structures interrelated to it. Reciprocally, it analyzes the way the given structure is molded by other structures in the system. For example, in a Muslim society, religious institutions have a considerable impact on the nature of other institutions, such as education (its content, its preferential attention to education for boys, the role of the teacher), family (the rights and duties of family members, role of women, kinship), business (problems of money-lending, obligation). In turn, the religious institution Islam is a function of the many conditions of Middle Eastern life and circumstance. Deciding where to start examining the interrelated "structures" of a culture is almost a chicken-and-egg debate. Every culture has to have a certain degree of integration and mutual consistency among its parts if it is to serve adequately the group which practices the culture, and not come apart with impossible contradictions and inconsistencies. Hence, any institution tends to adapt to the cultural and social landscape in order to survive.

Such concepts as "system," "structure," and "function" are becoming the *lingua franca* of anthropologists, sociologists, and political scientists. This conceptual orientation for analyzing elements in social and cultural systems started with the anthropologists. Their patient studies of primitive societies gave them a unique vantage point. Over a period of time they have been able to know, describe, and catalogue virtually all the important institutions and supporting customs of many relatively uncomplicated cultures. They have been able to see cultures as integrated wholes. A good ethnographic report covers language, life cycle, kinship system, religious institutions, economic activity, mythology, art, even the construction of blow guns or canoes. There it is—all of it! As more ethnographic reports came in describing more simple cultures, comparative analysis became the next logical step. In seeking answers to the obvious contrasts found, anthropologists turned to analyzing the relationship of the parts of a culture to each other, and to the total cultural configuration. They found that kinship customs might be closely related to yam growing, to tribal organization, or to property ownership. Religion might take forms consistent with the circumstances and anxieties of primitive life in a tropical forest—or in a desert environment. Child-rearing practices produced the personalities necessary for living in psychological peace with the roles that adults must assume. In short, the anthropologist's advantage was being able to take a single culture, in effect draw a ring around it, and study the parts in a single system, an early kind of structure-function analysis. Few other social scientists have enjoyed this vantage point, and foreign affairs officers virtually never do.

What emerged was a conceptualization of society as a network of interwoven parts, with the meaning of any single item being derived from the nature of other items to which it was related. Thus anthropology changed from the study of strange and exotic customs to the study of the function of cultural items, i.e., to explaining a given custom or institution in terms of its functional interrelationship with the rest of a cultural system. This is "cultural relativity" at the sophisticated and analytical level. Anthropology, in its vanguard at least, changed from a classifying science to a dynamic inquiry into the structure and function of cultural systems. Rather than simply establish *what* the custom or institution was, anthropologists began to establish *why* it was that way, what the consequences of a particular practice would be in that cultural system, and how practices might change. This order of scientific inquiry was very different, and its results have had an important impact on the other social sciences.

The sociologists carried the functional interrelationship idea further. Robert Merton was specific on the subject, and started sociologists on the conceptual path of seeing institutions (or other "structures") as having *manifest* functions, i.e., those which are recognized and intended in the system, and *latent* functions, or consequences in the system which were not necessarily intended or even consciously recognized.[2] For example, the automobile industry not only provided more efficient transportation but it also led to changes in dating patterns, symbols of prestige, and the physical structure of cities. Some functions might even be *dysfunctional* according to Merton in that in an unintended way they produced negative consequences, or imbalance and lack of integration in the system. For instance, in some cases introducing efficient power machinery on large estates in traditional societies left the peasants without employment or livelihood; introducing computers and automation may do the same thing in more modern societies—dysfunctions at least in short-term consequences.

Talcott Parsons and his students and associates have attempted to provide concepts for analyzing social systems in greater detail, and for designating variables in functional interrelationships which can be empirically tested—the mission in life for many sociologists at the present time. For this reason Parsons' theory has had a great impact on sociology and political science in the last fifteen years.[3] In this development, political scientists especially have become the new converts.[4] Unfortunately, some of them tried to go too far too fast in applying empirical methodology to quantify and to manipulate mathematically variables derived from theoretical models inspired by the Parsonsian approach, and the results have been unimpressive to say the least. The researchers often rushed to the computer seeking correlations between factors which either had no reliable measurement in the first place, or lacked a prior logical framework for seeking correlations.

However, regardless of how well it can be tested, functional interrelationship has a broad conceptual application. In public diplomacy it helps explain how contrasting preconceptions are held for institutions, how institutions can be perceived and reacted to in differing ways, and how international communication about them is thereby complicated. People do not ordinarily pay conscious attention to the functional interrelationships among their institutions; the integrative capacity of normal cognitive processes does it for them outside their awareness. Thus the mind pulls together past experience and common knowledge which makes it feel "natural" to an American, let us say, to begin a Senate session with prayer (meshing governmental and religious institutions), to pass a law to protect the rights of small investors in the stock exchange (combining economic, legal, and social structure institutions), or provide luxury items in post exchanges when the troops go overseas (making military life as consistent as possible with the consuming habits of a society accustomed to the benefits of mass production institutions).

The functional approach is particularly useful in examining how well institutions can be transferred from one society to another, as in technical assistance or colonial administration, or, much to the point in times of ideological confrontation, the degree to which Western democratic institutions can be transferred to newly independent nations, which otherwise present great contrasts in cultural base.[5]

The practical applications of these theoretical methods may be seen more clearly in a somewhat more detailed example, a case study of the Philippines.

The Philippine Case

For the observer interested in comparing the characteristics of newly independent states according to the kind of colonial administration they have experienced, travel in Southeast Asia can be instructive. In a relatively small area, more or less similar in pre-colonial aspects, one can review the institutional aftermath of four administrations: the British in Malaya and Singapore; the French in Indochina; the Dutch in Indonesia; and the American in the Philippines. For contrast, one can consider Thailand, which has maintained an independent status. The case of the Philippines is especially significant, for over a period of almost fifty years American administrators were engaged in transporting American-style institutions to Philippine cultural soil. Today both Americans and Filipinos are seriously reviewing what has happened in this close association, and giving careful judgment to choosing the next steps in the relationship.

Including the technical assistance period since independence in 1946, Americans have been talking with Filipinos for the last 70 years about American and Philippine institutions. Generally they simply have not communicated with the same preconceptions or mental images of governmental, economic, educational, and other institutions. This has been especially true from the standpoint of the average citizen, but it has also been true among officials and those most directly concerned with public administration. This case is all the more forceful as it is a salient instance in which the United States has been the formal source or model for institutions to be adopted in a foreign area under its administration.

At the end of the Spanish-American war, Americans found, with some national embarrassment, that the Islands were under their control, and that the United States was a "colonial" power. Because of the historic American heritage of independence and self-determination, this situation posed problems. Although some "hawks" of that day welcomed it as evidence of America's growing world importance, this country sought to justify itself by setting forth with missionary zeal to bring Philippine institutions into line with the American's ethnocentric concepts of enlightenment and the democratic good life. Consequently, with the Islands' "pacification"—the history of which is less flattering than we like to recall—the U.S. government sent out administrators and teachers in considerable numbers to establish American institutions in the Philippines. Some of the teachers, known as the "Thomasites," after the U.S. Army transport which brought them to the Philippines in 1901, stayed on through World War II and survived even into the 1960s.

Under Governor William H. Taft and the Philippine Commission, the Americans introduced U.S. conceptions of municipal government, civil service, a congress, political parties, and a free press. The process is reported in full detail by William Cameron Forbes in his two-volume work, *The Philippine Islands,* published in 1928. The American viewpoint on undertaking the task was grandly described as follows: "The Commission, with their keen American minds, their sense of justice and dislike of delay, display, sham, and subterfuge, were turned loose upon a world of medieval mismanagement and abuse like a group of knight-errants looking for wrongs to right and abuses to end. They found plenty of these and literally worked themselves sick in their efforts to bring into the Islands the blessing of the kind of administration to which Americans have become so accustomed that they take it as a matter of course." [6]

Other spheres of life also received the U.S. stamp; over time such institutions as Protestant churches, labor unions, and the Boy Scouts became part of the Philippine scene. When independence was formalized in 1946, it was done, logically, on the Fourth of July.

Filipinos are not completely self-assured as a result of their Spanish, and then American tutelage. They complain that they have spent three hundred years in a convent followed by fifty years in Hollywood. In any case, the American visitor to the

Philippines today does see considerable survival of many American institutions, at least formally. Superficially he feels at home. The Philippines is largely a free society politically. The parties hold their national conventions and conduct popular political campaigns, and administrations change in accordance with the vote. Public schools extend to the farthest islands. The Boy Scouts have survived; there are also Rotary and Lions clubs. English is the language of education, government, and business. Editorials in the press will sometimes prove a point by quoting Lincoln or Jefferson.

Yet after all the years of U.S. control, plus twenty-five years of technical assistance since independence, and with thousands of Filipinos educated in the United States, the two countries are still discussing the structure and function of Filipino institutions, and the two views of the situation still do not coincide. Some American technicians still tend to express their viewpoint—and their exasperation—as Forbes did in 1928. Concerned Filipinos feel they may have tried too hard to follow U.S. models when other institutional forms might have fitted their needs and culture better. While many institutions have been transplanted *formally* in the Philippines, the full *conception* or image of these institutions which makes them function as they do in the United States has not been transplanted, and perhaps cannot be, since conceptions—idea patterns, role expectations, assumptions regarding the function of an institution—are rooted in the psychocultural base of the larger society and in its total way of life. Even if Americans tried to transfer all their supporting conceptions abroad intact, they would be hard pressed to know just what they are, since some of the basic elements are normally beyond their own awareness. As Forbes said, Americans "take it as a matter of course." The problem is compounded as any receiving society, such as the Philippines, supplies to the transplanted institutions its own set of conceptions about government, education, social structure, and the function of institutions. Hence, communication problems have persisted.

The Philippine education system is an institution in point. Before the arrival of the Americans, education was formal, religiously oriented, confined to an elite, and closely related to social prestige. The academic title was a symbol of social status. With the American idea of universal education, access to education was indeed expanded; humble Filipinos aspired to education as never before. But the mental images and set of expectations surrounding the function of education did not change quickly. The school certificate or the academic degree itself was seen as the objective rather than the content of the educational process. In higher education law and medicine were the preferred fields, as these degrees carried traditional social prestige. With a new pressure for degrees, private schools and universities sprang up as profit-making enterprises catering to the popular demand. They often operated as uninhibited diploma mills, for the public had little appreciation of what quality in education meant, or how the educational process might fit the young man or woman for employment or professional competence. In light of what was said above about the functional interrelationship factors determining the basis for perceiving and responding to institutions, it is clear that the Philippine educational system became a substantially different institution from the Stateside model.

The communication gulf persisted into the 1960s. Each new specialist arrived in the Philippines convinced that education would produce the magic development the Islands wanted and needed—a view not too different from that of the Thomasites at the turn of the century. Since the educational system was still not functioning in the image of the technician's professional standards, more local teacher training was provided, funds were made available for buildings and equipment, more grants were given for travel in the United States. But the real institutional problem has been met only slowly, as teachers and the larger society have changed their subtle set of mental patterns regarding schools and universities, changed priorities in value systems, and realized that degrees in engineering lead to better jobs than in the surfeited field of law. Today young Filipinos themselves are adding pressure for a more rational Philippine-oriented system. The optimum educational institution will not be a carbon copy of a U.S. system, but an institution which can be better integrated into Philippine society and culture. But after seventy years of almost continual purposive effort, *the Philippine educational institution is essentially a Philippine institution* in all but its formal structure, organizational charts, and instructors' manuals!

Similar conclusions could be reached for many other transplanted institutions, with government institutions high on the list. The Philippine military institution is modern and sophisticated, and has many successful ventures to its credit. Yet it is a substantially different institution from the United States Army, Navy, or Air Force, in spite of years of U.S.-oriented military training, starting with the Philippine Scouts, extending through cooperation during World War II, and since the war through the use of U.S. advisors, military equipment, and all the corresponding manuals and technical organization charts. So, too, the police system, judiciary, political parties, and cabinet offices. Economic institutions such as banks, hotels, the stock market, publishing companies—even organized crime—display all-important differences when their function and attendant assumptions and preconceptions are considered, despite formal similarities to their American counterparts.

The purpose of this discussion is not to judge what *should* be the outcome of this instance of extensive cross-cultural borrowing, but to call attention to the part of the iceberg below the surface which determines the impediments to communication about institutions between Americans and Filipinos. In the first place, there is a difference in social structure. In the Philippines there is less of a middle class; the population is just now coming into nearly universal literacy; the nation is subdivided into rival regional groups generally divided along the lines of a half-dozen major language groups and dozens of minor ones. The government started with a tradition of strong centralization; local initiative was not the usual way to get things done, and there were few "states' rights." The landholding system in parts of the islands has tended to perpetuate a cleavage between the influential wealthy families and the peasants, which at its worst represented outright exploitation and at its best benign paternalism. Much of commerce has been concentrated in the hands of the Chinese, a minority only partly assimilated into Philippine society and culture. The physical and moral destruction of World War II, the Japanese occupation, and the demands for survival through the war and the early postwar era have left a degree of social disorganization.

The tasks facing Philippine government institutions are typical of developing countries—immediate needs in housing, highways, power, communications, and social services. The Filipino bureaucrat has to be most optimistic to think that they will be met successfully in a short time. This fact in itself greatly changes the functional requirements of Philippine government institutions as compared with those in the United States, where the society places very different demands on corresponding agencies.

Philippine society has its components of modal personality or national character which influence the way in which institutions operate. High value is placed on personal and family loyalties, and on honoring reciprocal obligations. These attitudes tend to be the value orientations which hold the society together. There remains today a certain fatalistic outlook known as *bahala na* (so be it), which, while slowly changing, still affects the citizen's expectations of himself and of his government.

Over all this is the fact that the Philippines has been on its own as a national society for barely a generation, after centuries of having its affairs censured and supervised by a foreign power. There are problems in psychological integration as the society settles on such matters as national identity, the emotional and philosophical basis by which Filipinos in authority are expected to exercise authority over other Filipinos, and the symbols of national pride and national values which can serve to unify the nation in its difficult endeavors.

Taking the above considerations as a starting point, and recognizing that these differing factors are basic elements in the psychological worlds or cognitive structures of the average Filipino, it is evident that for Filipinos institutions must operate on differing preconceptions and subjective meanings than for Americans. Logically, their perceptions and response to our programs in institutional change will have a uniquely Filipino dimension which, in the end, will be the all-important one.

V

Language, Perception,

and Reasoning

Precision in using language is, of course, essential to the conduct of foreign affairs. Even before trying to cross language barriers, the diplomat must draft cables and dispatches to his government in his own language so that there can be no mistake in meaning. He must be precise in expressing his and his government's position to the foreign office to which he is accredited, and to the press and public. The need to speak foreign languages and the demand for accurate translation—even instantaneous translation in international conferences and elsewhere—is elementary. But language can complicate international communication and public diplomacy in certain additional persistent ways, often beyond our awareness, which are less professionally appreciated despite their importance. The basic question is how realistic are we when we assume that communication, in its broad dimension of perception and reasoning, can be fully achieved when a translation must be made.

We will pursue implications of language differences which go somewhat beyond semantics and the usual considerations which go with the study of meaning and connotation of words. Most people who are working seriously in international relations are well aware of the semantics component in communications problems, so it would not be particularly useful to duplicate or summarize the extensive materials already available in this field. Well-known sources include S. I. Hayakawa's *Language in Thought and Action*,[1] and Stuart Chase's *Power of Words*.[2]

Indeed the significance of semantics implications can hardly be overestimated. One example of its importance is given by Stuart Chase, who cites W. J. Coughlin's account (in a 1953 issue of *Harpers*) of the consequences of the Japanese word *mokusatsu* having two meanings: "to ignore," and "to refrain from comment." According to this review of the final phase of World War II, the Japanese cabinet in 1945 was preparing to accept the Allies' Potsdam ultimatum to surrender, but wanted more time to discuss terms. Their press release announced a policy of *mokusatsu*, meaning "no comment." But a translation supplied the other meaning, which implied that the cabinet was "ignoring" the ultimatum. The domestic situation was already delicate, and once the release had reached the public, it would have been too embarrassing to correct the error and, in effect, draw attention to the more compliant meaning. Had the Japanese cabinet not found itself out on this semantics limb, it is speculated, they might have backed up the Emperor's decision to surrender at that time; the atomic bomb might not have been used in Japan, Russian armies might not have come to Manchuria, and there might not have been a Korean war! [3]

Language: A Master Framework for Perception

How much do language and language structure affect the way in which people perceive issues and events and determine their meaning? Does language predispose the perceiver to use particular reasoning processes from which responses are generated? To what extent is one's psychological world—or cognitive processes—a function of language? To what extent is this factor completely bridged by translation?

The role which language plays in the very existence of culture and of structured human relationships is absolutely essential. Language is the most important means by which what one man learns is transmitted to another, including transmission from generation to generation, so that culture is cumulative wisdom and experience. It is man's mechanism for cooperation and division of labor, for accomplishing things which one man could not do alone. In short, language is the essential attribute of humans which separates them from the lesser animals; it is the key element which allows man to adapt to his environment despite his relatively unimpressive physical equipment—unimpressive except for a prehensile hand and a brain which backs up his use of language.

Even without language, man would have some limited degree of memory, but no ability to pass on to other humans what is in his memory, his ideas, or what he is experiencing. Within his own mental processes, even if he did not try to communicate with other men, to what extent could he think his thoughts or engage in any abstract reasoning without a language framework to channel his cognitive functions? As few humans exist without having some exposure to language, it would be hard to conduct any empirical investigation to resolve this question, and besides, without language such a person could not communicate much of what was going on in his mind. At the least it is apparent that the relationship between language and reasoning is an intimate one. From the time a human infant begins to distinguish the features of his world, the relationships and roles of the people around him, and begins to form some conception of himself, he does so by using the words and language patterns which are supplied him by the human society in which he is cared for and "socialized." The process continues through life; new knowledge, ideas, and other people's experience come to the human's attention mostly in the form of language.

This is acceptable enough. But then we come to the key question: Does it make any difference *which* language? Can the same thoughts and patterns of reasoning take place in any language, or are they likely to? Or do differing language structures, word concepts, and ways of categorizing experience lead to selective perception processes of the kind discussed in Chapter II? If language is so intimately tied up with thought and reasoning, do different languages set the stage for differing formulae in cognitive processes? Do different languages represent—right from the beginning —different psychological worlds? If they do, then any understanding of the perception and response factor in foreign affairs must include the role which language plays because we are suggesting that the perception and reasoning processes which produce responses in foreign affairs may already be partly preprogrammed by the guiding rails of language on which thoughts, perceptions, thinking, and reasoning must run. We would also be suggesting that exact and full communication across a language translation might be impossible unless the two languages involved provide the same design for categorizing experiences and structuring thought.

Early theorizing on the subject, at least in the Western tradition, seems to have been that of Aristotle, or perhaps more accurately of the school of logic and philosophy which bears his name. His was a negative case. His school conceived of thought and logic as being universal once the principles are discovered. In this conception, words were merely mechanisms, or something of a dealer's choice in expressing an essence of being and reasoning which all men, or at least all educated men, share. Hence, reality and reasoning about reality are considered universal in nature and in application, and unaffected by language. The same truth should be apparent to all men. This assumption has survived for a long time. It still seems to be an unconscious assumption behind many an official information or propaganda program. In fact, more than once American officials have been pressured into using Madison Avenue advertising techniques as models for information programs which must cross cultural and linguistic barriers. In other words, it is supposed that what appeals to reason at home must appeal everywhere.

Especially as applied to science, this Aristotelian outlook has suffered a series of rude shocks over the centuries. The "universal reality" from which deductions could be made had to be modified with Galileo, and again with Einstein. Around 1940, the Aristotelian view of language also suffered a "theory of relativity" challenge when anthropologists began concerning themselves with languages used in societies far removed from the conventions of Western culture.[4]

In anthropology, credit for starting a new approach to studying the relationship between language and thought has gone mostly to Benjamin Lee Whorf, and to a lesser extent to his mentor, Edward Sapir. By vocation Whorf was an engineer; he was an M.I.T. graduate and a specialist in fire prevention for the Hartford Fire Insurance Company. By dedicated avocation he was a linguistic scientist. He became particularly interested in the Hopi language, and in the strikingly different ways in which Hopi words and expressions seem to conceptualize things, events, even the cosmos. For example, Hopi provides no conception of "time" as a continuum as it is so elaborately conceived in English, but handles it more as duration related to specific actions or events. Events occur without designated causal agents tied to verbs and predicates; verbs have no tenses. The product of his observations is to be found, rather disjointedly presented, in various published articles which together amount to a hypothesis regarding the relationship between language and thought. Stuart Chase summarizes this hypothesis in a foreword to a collection of Whorf's writings entitled *Language, Thought, and Reality*.[5] He says Whorf came to believe that "all higher levels of thinking are dependent on language," and "that the structure of the language one habitually uses influences the manner in which one understands his environment." Therefore, "the picture of the universe shifts from tongue to tongue." Or, as Whorf states it in one of his articles ("Science and Linguistics," 1940): "We are thus introduced to a new principle of relativity, which holds that all observers are not led by the same physical evidence to the same picture of the universe, unless their linguistic backgrounds are similar, or can in some way be calibrated." [6]

Psychologists have attempted to verify the Whorf hypothesis experimentally, especially as it refers to physical perception. For example, when languages categorize the color spectrum in different ways, do people actually tend to perceive colors differently? The evidence is mixed, particularly when the psychologist tries to determine whether the subject is actually unaware of color differences as they reach his senses, or whether he simply has to comply with the arbitrary color definitions which his language provides to report what he sees. As human visual equipment seems to be essentially the same from group to group, people seem to be able to distinguish physically one shade or intensity from another in about the same degree. But the way they categorize what they see does differ, and in turn the distinctions they notice as significant tend to follow their linguistic habits for categorizing colors. Further, there seems to be a clear connection between the word divisions of colors available and efficiency in remembering colors seen in the experiments.

To the extent that careful analysis has been carried out in cases of social perception, the experimental evidence clearly supports Whorf. That is, people do perceive events in social situations, social relationships, roles, and even their own behavior differently as language differences conceptualize such matters in differing ways. In general, it appears that the more abstract the subject to be perceived, the more language differences can affect the perception.[7]

According to evidence available from the observations and analyses of semanticists, anthropologists working on comparative modal personality, translators and interpreters, and from those engaged in research on the normal and abnormal functions of the human brain, the importance of language difference in predisposing cognitive processes to operate in differing ways is sufficiently established to demand attention in the foreign affairs field. As evidence on the lighter side, the following was reported by a young lady of French descent who worked as a secretary in a government office in a newly independent country in North Africa. Staff meetings were held in either Arabic or French, or the men assembled might switch from one language to the other according to the subject. When the secretary had occasion to enter the room while they were speaking in French, they would always courteously rise. If, however, they were speaking Arabic, they ignored her completely. At least there seems to be *some* relationship between a language used and a feeling of being in the culture world of that language!

Some association between language and perception is found at the semantics and connotation level. In line with what we know about perception in general, it would be expected that as the connotation of words varies in different cultures or even in sub-cultures typical perception patterns would be expected to vary also even when the words are generally equivalent in denotation in both languages. Norman Cousins pointed out in an editorial note in the *Saturday Review* [8] that a language research team found that most of the 120 synonyms for black in English in standard thesaurus sources were negative, including such items as sinister, evil, wicked, and malignant. Of 134 synonyms for white, almost all were favorable in connotation, including pure, honorable, and trustworthy. Yellow carried some predominantly negative connotations such as coward, conniver, or sneak. The racial implications when these words are used in English is fairly obvious whether or not their use corresponds with actual variation in pigmentation. Cousins noted that other cultures add their own connotations. In Chinese, while whiteness means cleanliness, it can "also mean bloodlessness, coldness, frigidity, absence of feeling, weakness, insensitivity." Yellowness may be associated with "sunshine, openness, beauty, flowering." In many African languages, black connotes "strength, certainty, recognizability and integrity, while white is associated with paleness, anemia, unnaturalness, deviousness, untrustworthiness."

v / *Language, Perception, and Reasoning*

Cross-cultural contrasts in the connotation of words which are used routinely in translation present an obvious impediment to communication—an impediment which is usually ignored. Lorand B. Szalay and his associates have developed an objective technique for establishing just what these contrasts are for key words and concepts, and have developed prototype lexicons which can be applied to practical translation problems such as those found in bilingual training or advisory programs, civil information and public relations activities, or news dissemination.[9]

Their method was to select pairs of words or concepts which are accepted equivalents in translation. Then they selected a sample of native speakers from each language group and asked them to make brief but sustained free associations with the stimulus word in their language. Their written responses were tabulated and analyzed statistically, and salient connotative components were isolated. In some cases both the reference and the intensity of the connotative components turned out to be similar, but usually there were significant differences. For example, in English the connotation of "government official" stresses public service; and the image includes elected officials like the president and congressmen, along with the military and the police. The connotation of the Korean equivalent (*kwalli*) places relatively more emphasis on the range of functions which officials perform, on their position and power, and on the appointment process. It brought to mind a greater degree of unfavorable association with graft and corruption. Elected officials were less likely to be thought of in the same category. The concept "national interest" evoked relatively low intensity responses from the English-speaking group, and their associations centered around goals and ideals, national defense, the role of leaders in promoting the public interest, people, and the interests of people, such as sports. The Korean equivalent (*kykka iik*) evoked a stronger response, but one expressed more in economic terms: development, national income, trade, industry, and production.

Going through a series of key concepts in such a lexicon is not only a study in communication but in cultural differences as well. Statistical techniques for making analyses of this kind have been available for a long time. It is surprising that it was not until the late 1960s that a project so obviously pertinent to communication across language barriers was undertaken.

On a more philosophical level, Salvador de Madariaga makes frequent reference in his classic *Englishmen, Frenchmen, Spaniards* to word concepts which are used as the best translations among the three languages spoken, but which in fact represent different perceptions or orientations to society and to events, different concepts of man himself, and different representations of the intellectual process typical of the three cultures. Thus, the English "to be right" is translated into French as *avoir raison*. De Madariaga judges that the two represent quite different viewpoints. "To be right" is a quality or vital state of the body like being well or sick. But for the French to "have" or hold reason as a possession is consistent with the French concern with the intellectual process, with logic, and with law—which also is not quite the same in the French word *droit* as in the English "law." To de Madariaga, the Englishman is a man of action and of empirical investigation rather than deductive speculation, a man whose thought must pragmatically relate to a real world at hand. Thus "to be right" is a state, or condition to be described as such.[10] Can we be sure that when it is translated as *avoir raison* it represents an equivalent thought?

Anthropologists have long observed that as circumstances demand more exact perception and communication about essential elements of a culture, the language accommodates. English provides thousands of words for dealing with gasoline motors, parts and equipment, electronic gear and its operation, and the technology of medical science. Most of these words would be unnecessary in a simpler culture, and would be lacking, of course. On the other hand, Arabic supplies thousands of words for camels, camel equipment, and a camel's peculiar characteristics. There are some sixty words dealing just with pregnant camels.

Arabic provides the means for detailed conceptions of all that goes on in relation to camels in a culture where survival itself once depended on just such careful perception and understanding of the camel. Most of this fine distinction would escape the European or American, even when face to face with a camel. To them, camels would be pretty much the same; male or female, perhaps, tall or short, brown or grey, one hump or two. There would be no need to be more precise.

Anthropologists note that cultures differ widely in words and concepts used for family relationships, some of which extend into clan and tribal organization. They find that the terminology used tends to be consistent with the local social need to perceive roles and relationships. French, German, and Spanish require the speaker to make a distinction in address between familiar and more formal relationships; English uses "you" to cover the entire range, and accordingly does not predispose the speaker to fix attention on the kind of relationship he enjoys with the person spoken to. Japanese contains a very long list of honorifics—words which make fine distinctions in status or obligation in interpersonal relationships. The Japanese perceive these distinctions habitually, and take them seriously. In Chinese you must distinguish between elder brother and younger brother—it always made more difference there, and probably still does despite the superimposition of Communist ideology.

The Western mind has always had difficulty with Chinese thought. We do not know just how much Chinese and Western perceptions of the world differ, but features of the Chinese language suggest that the difference might be considerable. Spoken and written Chinese use entirely different means to symbolize and conceptualize the world and its events. Written Chinese characters may contain a whole complex of concepts in a single pictogram or ideogram. Even a phonogram is complicated because many different spoken words have essentially the same pronunciation except for stress and tone. The sequence of written characters follows the order in which the ideas occur to the writer rather than the fixed mold of sentence structure found in Indo-European languages.

Spoken Chinese itself is a highly distinct way of categorizing and subdividing experience. It started out as a monosyllabic language, and remains so to a large extent. That is, words tend to be simple, but there are very numerous designations of all the discrete items and their variations in perceived experience. Words are not normally inflected to accommodate to differing grammatical use, and standing alone they cannot be classified as parts of speech. Whether a word acts as a noun or a verb depends on the context and the intention. If the context is clear, a single word may carry the meaning adequately. If not, further words are added to round out the meaning or to make its reference more precise. Thus additional words may specify such matters as gender, the time of action, or other pertinent considerations. Western languages tend to summarize or categorize elements in the universe, while Chinese calls attention to the infinite variety in all things. Modern compounding of words and habitual combinations reduce the apparent contrast in the way the Chinese tongues seem to package ideas. Still, the language remains distinctly enigmatic to Westerners, affects the way in which the Chinese compose ideas in English when they use it as a second language, and, in the final analysis, reflects a somewhat different pattern of conceptualizing the world and its events.[11]

As written Chinese found its way into Korea and Japan when the peoples in both countries already had quite unrelated spoken languages, it is interesting to speculate on the mixture of conceptualizations and patterns of reasoning which must have resulted. The Japanese have found the written language unsuitable for modern science and technology, especially as they have added new words from the West which go along with new concepts. They have made strenuous efforts to reduce some of the inconsistency and have tried to adopt a more phonetic system. But the written language and the intellectual habits which grew with it have existed for many generations, and tend to resist change.

Whether culture or words came first to cause the other is hard to determine, and may not be the issue. The practical fact is that they are intimately associated, and that, as we suggested above, when a child begins to perceive his world and internalize his characteristic patterns of reasoning, he does so in terms of the word categories and linguistic ways of connecting ideas made available to him by the language of his group. Curiously, little study has been made of what happens when a child goes through this process in two widely differing languages at once, and becomes bilingual from the time he starts to use language. Does such a person think normally in one language to the exclusion of the other? Sometimes in one, and sometimes in another, depending on the subject and context of the thoughts? Or does he just think thoughts? When such a person is asked about it, he has to stop and consider, and I have found little consistency in the answers from one respondent to the next. Does such a person enjoy a greater breadth of perception and a more ample field for reasoning by having available the thought structures of two languages? Or does the personality, in its need to achieve internal consistency and integration, avoid such division? Does such a person live in two different psychological worlds, switching from one to the other as he switches languages?

When the second language is learned later, the evidence is clearer. It depends somewhat on the circumstances under which the second language was learned, but the tendency is to think along the lines established by the habits of the first and to make the second language conform as well as possible to its idea patterns. Thus, when a person is speaking a second language, we become aware that it is not only the accent which indicates he is not a native speaker, but also *what he chooses to try to say.*

It is interesting to observe Africans or Asians who have been educated in English or French—the education itself adding an additional component to the association between language and culture. Such a bilingual person will often step from one psychological world to another as he crosses the social worlds of the two languages. He often expresses quite different ideas in the two languages. The political leader may reason in one way when talking with his own people, in another when talking in a foreign language with a foreign diplomat. Some observers believe that Nasser's inconsistencies in foreign policy statements could be explained this way.

Obviously it is extremely difficult to isolate language as a variable in the total interplay of factors which go into perception and reasoning processes, especially when dealing with the abstract subjects which are usual in foreign affairs communications. Cause and effect are hard to establish. In presenting this line of questioning in this chapter, I do not pose as an expert. Yet it seems that some language differences may almost force differing patterns of perceiving on a person. Or, if that judgment is too strong, it appears that language differences do lead to differing *habits* of perceiving and reasoning which, in international communication, produce the same result. In reviewing the evidence, it seems that these differing habits are produced at three general levels of association between language and thinking ("association" is sufficient without prematurely stating cause and effect): (1) the level of differing content; (2) the level of differing choice in conceptualizing subjects and events, whether because the language requires it or because people by habit choose one way of saying something over another; and (3) the level of language structure itself and the differing ways in which languages tend to bring ideas and concepts together in precast formats for logic, reasoning, memory, and abstract thinking.

Language Content and Perception

This level is easy and obvious. Since any language reflects its culture, its translatability or comparability with another language depend on the translatability of the culture itself. Or, as we have emphasized, since culture can be interpreted to consist in the final analysis largely of patterns of the mind, translation depends on comparability of knowledge, beliefs, assumptions, daily concerns, and interests. Vocabulary content varies accordingly.

We have mentioned motors, camels, and kinship. Anthropologists have noticed that while most Americans, except ski enthusiasts, perhaps, fare reasonably well with one general word for snow, certain Eskimo languages cannot operate with such an imprecise generality, even with modifying words. Hence they have no simple word for "snow." Is the snow hard or soft, old or new, crystalline or fine powder? It is as though the various states of snow were not the same substance, just as ice is not water. More exact words exist for the Eskimo, consistent with his need to perceive the exact nature of the snow.

We often find that although substantially equivalent ideas can be expressed in two languages, what is said efficiently and directly in one short word in one language may require a whole phrase in another. To be exact we might have to say in English "my aunt on my father's side," or perhaps "my father's sister." In many other languages where relationships are taken more seriously, there is a single word to designate that relationship, and only that relationship. There seems to be a correlation between the shortness of a word and how specific it is, and its importance and frequency of use. On the other hand, a word may be short enough, but be very general, like "snow" or "aunt." If one must add words to narrow the focus and be more specific, this indicates that the society most frequently uses a general conception of the subject. Speakers of a language using the more general reference are not necessarily unable to think or perceive in terms of the finer distinctions provided by a language which offers more specific terminology. But they must make more effort to do so, or perhaps they do not normally do so. It is apparent that the speaker of the more specific terminology is more attuned to perceiving the distinctions which his vocabulary asks him to make. The child learns his perception habits in the vocabulary frame of reference offered, further reinforcing the association between vocabulary and perception.

Diffusion of artifacts and customs from one culture to another will call for corresponding linguistic adjustment, and a study of word origins can reflect the history of a culture. I once spent several months with the Otomí Indians in the state of Hidalgo, Mexico. One of my favorite pastimes was to try to find out what items were part of Otomí culture before the Spanish arrived from the present-day names of the items. When the item was the maguey plant, corn, various tools, parts of their huts, some items of clothing, the word for it was usually distinctly Otomí. When the item was a cow, burro, metal tool, a book, certain vegetables, it was something identifiable with Spanish, if not the Spanish word itself. The correlation was not perfect, but the pattern was clear. In fact, this method is used to trace the movement and mixing of peoples which took place before history produced more direct evidence.

With modern technology, languages around the world have tended to become more similar. Radio, television, baseball, generator, atom bomb are incorporated in many languages intact, or with phonetic adjustment to suit local tastes. Diplomacy itself has contributed certain international diplomatic usages to serve its needs and reduce misunderstandings. The advertising campaigns of international distributors of goods and services also have added to an international common denominator in languages. It is hard to travel beyond the realm of Coca Cola, Sony, Singer, and Volkswagen.

International communication is understandably complicated when an idea exists in one culture and not in another. Some of them have considerable significance in international affairs. For instance, "fair play" is a peculiarly English phrase, and denotes an idea pattern peculiar to the English and their cultural offspring. It has no original counterpart in French or Spanish. The

French now use *le fer plé*. In fact, it has no exact equivalent in most languages—it is an idea that is native to Anglo-Saxon value systems and conceptualizations of relationships among contestants, of the nature of competition, and the ethics of winning and losing. It applies not only to the sports world but also to politics and even to warfare. It is interesting to note that in Latin America, where the forms of many American democratic institutions have been adopted, including the election process, it is only recently and only in certain countries that the side which loses an election will agree that the result was other than fraud, will swallow its honor, and in good grace congratulate the winner—in the spirit of fair play. Passions in the soccer stadium are another world! [12]

On the other hand, the Latin Americans have concepts which have no exact equivalents in English. *Dignidad,* which we would translate as "dignity," has a more special meaning, which combines a Latin American concept of personal worth with highly-valued individuality—special personal qualities, personal honor, and uniqueness of person regardless of one's station in life. It is a value orientation which underlies social relationships and gives logic to manners and fulfillment of obligations. Great emphasis is placed on protecting one's *dignidad* if one is to maintain social respectability; correspondingly many social customs serve to avoid situations in which a person's *dignidad* might be vulnerable, or to redress the situation when *dignidad* is wounded. Thus we have a clash of concepts: one may borrow the election process, but it is hard to borrow the fair play idea along with it, for it is difficult to take a fair play attitude when one's *dignidad* is at stake. Even in the deliberations of such sophisticated and cosmopolitan organizations as the United Nations, such contrasting viewpoints affect parliamentary proceedings and call for a special facility in intercultural diplomacy. One might note the similar problem with the word "compromise." In English it might add to one's dignity to compromise, but not in Spanish.

Another example is the idea "public interest." Several years ago a group of technicians in public administration working in Pakistan attempted to have a manual translated for local officials. When they found that this term defied translation into Urdu, they began to see why their concept of the "public" was failing to get across as they had intended. The concept "public" appears not to be universal, even though there are "publics" everywhere. This is the kind of problem the political scientists are attempting to solve when they talk about "civic culture."

Conversely, the word "capitalism" is found in many languages, for in most cases it was simply taken over complete with dictionary definition from its origins in European economic thought. However, since the word was coined much has happened in different times and places, so that now the ideas denoted by it vary considerably around the world. It has been altered particularly in the United States, where the general economic practice which Americans think of as capitalism has been much affected by other democratic institutions in an open-class, achievement-oriented, honor-the-underdog society. It was further modified with the prompting of social consciousness in the 1930s and since, with much of the actual operation of the American system, particularly as government is involved, taking on a cast that would be called democratic socialism in other countries. But it is still "capitalism" to us, and as we try to communicate with the rest of the world, we tend to be unconscious of just how nearly unique American capitalism is, and how our use of the term simply does not stand up well in translation. The problem is made more difficult in that the Communist world has also taken the word rather far from its original meaning and added connotations of its own. In ideological debate they clash with the connotations from the United States.[13]

Other political terms used in current international communication are similarly loaded, including "democracy," "development," and "aggression." We will have more to say about this in the next chapter. The point here is that the kind of perception which we can expect to be stimulated by words, and the reasoning and response process which follows will depend heavily on understood meaning relative to cultural reference points. Thus direct translation, even officially certified translation accomplished by experts, only opens the door in international communication. It requires a considerable amount of cross-cultural empathy to capture shifts in connotation and nuance and to follow what is actually going on in what is supposed to be "communication."

Language May Conceptualize Actions and Events in Different Ways

The second suggested level of approach to language and perception is even more interesting in its implications, although somewhat more elusive. It is not completely distinct from the first level but it is more related to action and events, and represents a higher degree of abstraction in its effect on perception and cognitive processes. Consider the way an identical event is expressed in English and in Spanish. Let us say that a ball falls from a person's hand. In English he would probably say "I dropped the ball." In Spanish, the usual translation, and, in fact, the expression which normally would be used is *se me cayo la pelota*. Literally, this is nearer to "The ball fell from me." This is not the same conceptualization of what happened. Responsibility has shifted from the person to the ball!

This kind of shift in conceptualization takes place all the time in routine translations, for as a language provides a means of describing events, actions, and experiences, it inevitably provides only a limited selection of conceptualizations from which the speaker can choose, at least without going into modifying explanations. Further, among alternative conceptualizations available, the speaker will tend to choose the most customary expression. That is, he will follow his group's conventional choice of expression. Someone learning English might say, "The ball dropped from me," but he would be told that while he is grammatically correct, "We don't say it that way." Between the limits in choice of conceptualization set by a given language and the limits set by conventional expression, one's habitual ways of conceptualizing the actions and events around him become rather narrow in light of the many ways in which specific actions and events can be conceptualized in the world's many uses of language.

However, even after we recognize that language habits do demonstrate differing conceptualizations when one stops to examine them closely, the important question is whether this difference has any significance in perception and reasoning. Is the Latin American *really* thinking differently about the relationship between the ball and the person who had been holding it when he says *se me cayo?* After all, anyone who saw what happened knows the extent to which the ball was hard to handle, or the person was careless. We do intentionally make statements in English to imply that the ball can be the active agent; in baseball we blame the player less when we say, "The ball got away from the shortstop." When such differences in conceptualization are repeated and when they appear in patterns, there is at least reason to suspect that there are also differences in habitual perception, and that such potential differences deserve much closer attention than they are normally given by people working cross-culturally. *Se me cayo* does fit into a pattern of Latin American expression. Spanish speakers are far more inclined to use reflexive verbs and passive voice, while English speakers tend to use an active expression which presents events as results of the action of a personalized agent. The Spanish speaker uses subjunctive and conditional modes of expression more, in effect softening the harsh responsibility of the actor for the consequences of his actions.

It has, in fact, been argued that there is a patterned difference in the way that Americans and Latin Americans perceive the relationship between the individual and events or results of action. The traditional American tends to take the optimistic view that the world about him and its events are subject to man's intervention and manipulation. He sees himself as a causal agent who can move mountains, conquer cancer, and seed clouds to produce rain. The traditional Latin American, on the other hand, is more fatalistic. As we noted in Chapter II, he sees the world and its events as unalterable circumstances to which he must adjust. Or, if conditions are subject to change, they are influenced by powerful forces out of his direct control; the individual might be able to affect the outcome by pleading with a higher authority who can do something about it all. The orientation is such that the individual is less inclined to consider himself responsible for what happened—*se me cayo*—the ball fell, I was just standing here. Choice of conceptualization and outlook are consistent. But the American, faced with a problem says: "Don't just stand there. Do something!" He does "drop the ball." Thornton Wilder must have sensed this difference in some depth when he wrote the novel, *The Bridge of San Luis Rey*. The action takes place in Latin America. The story is a study of fatalism and people's sense of it when a bridge over a canyon gives way and carries several of the principal characters to their deaths. What did fate have in mind?

Another more subtle example, possibly of doubtful validity in arguing contrasting perception, is the usual translation of the English word "business" to *negocio* in Spanish. It offers grounds for interesting speculation. The English word is positive and connotes busyness, being busy, going about one's business, attending to one's business and not loafing. In Spanish, the value appears to be placed the other way around. The key is *ocio*, valued leisure, serenity, time to enjoy and contemplate. When harsh reality prevents one from enjoying his *ocio*, when it is negated, he must attend to his *negocio*. This interpretation was first given to me by a Latin American intellectual. In practical affairs the difference in implied conceptualization may be too small to make a difference. The word *negocio* has long roots, and a "negate leisure" connotation, which may have been valid in an earlier day may now be psychologically dead, but it does make one wonder whether "business" translates fully into *negocio*. The reader familiar with other foreign languages will be reminded of many similar examples.

Edmund Glenn offers an approach which may be helpful when the accepted translation may be subject to an underlying difference in conceptualization. He suggests that the "immediate" meaning may be clear enough, but that the "latent" meaning, which may make a difference in behavior at a later moment or in another aspect of the relationship between the speakers, is the subtle component which deserves attention.[14]

Again, we are plagued by the question does language *cause* perceptions to tend in one direction or another to become the habitual thought of a people, or does the choice of conceptualization in the language simply follow the thought habits of the culture? And again, we can settle for the significance of the *association*. However, as the language goes on from generation to generation we are back to the effect on the child who, on learning the characteristic perceptions suggested by his language, finds it easier and more logical to internalize the perception habits of his society than if he were learning to perceive in another language.

As occasion demands, new words and conceptualizations are coined precisely to express new perceptions or evaluations of experience and events, and they do in fact lead their users to new perceptions. The current youth culture in the United States has supplied a number of these. A person is "up tight." Someone is "straight." The existing order of things is the "establishment."

Language, then, presents a suggestive framework which leads the user to prefer one conceptualization over another. The choice of examples is nearly endless since more than 200 major languages and their many dialects are spoken in the world today.

The way in which time is conceptualized is often significant, as Whorf found in Hopi. In English, time is presented as a continuum. There is a ready supply of words and verb forms which allow—even force—one to place events precisely on this continuum, which has started in the unimaginable past, which "waits for no man," and which extends inexorably into the future with the ticking of a clock. Time is handled like an expensive commodity. It can be saved, wasted, made up, bought, and sold. Abusing time is censured; making good use of time is a virtue. But this conceptualization is not universal. Chinese expressions reflect less compulsion about time; they give much less importance to the present and are less concerned with determining the exact termination of events now in progress. This attitude is consistent with the current Chinese concept of revolution, which, like time, is a process; the direction of the process is relatively more important than the scheduled arrival time. Arabic has no future tense comparable with English. The future is in the hands of Allah; humans have little reason to speculate about it. In fact, the strict Muslim might consider the American's constant concern for the future immoral. Thus in perceiving events and reasoning about them, the speaker of Arabic might place relatively more attention on the immediate situation, and less on planning ahead or on considering the consequences which tomorrow might bring.

A society's ethics and its value systems are often revealed by the way it expresses approval or disapproval of behavior. When a small boy has misbehaved, in English, his mother might say something like, "John, you are a naughty boy. Be good." In French she might choose to say *sois sage,* be wise or sensible rather than foolish. In German, *sei artig,* be well behaved. And in Hopi, the expression would be, "No, no, that is not the Hopi way." The boy's actions are censured quite differently in each language. The expressions range from charging him with immoral behavior to reminding him that he is not in tune with his group. Thus the language, or typical choice of language, reinforces a concept of the act. It helps the child internalize the way in which his society perceives and evaluates his action. Thus he goes through the socialization process.[15]

American speakers of English use a variety of expressions reflecting the so-called sin-guilt complex, which derives from a

Puritan-influenced heritage: "He is a bad boy." "I feel guilty about it." "His conscience is bothering him." "I try to do the right thing." The implication is that the individual is competing against an impersonal moral standard, and that his ethics are internalized concepts of right and wrong, which go with him everywhere. While he may be censured by his fellowmen, he is ultimately on his own before divine judgment.

Latin American Spanish would allow one to say much the same thing, and a parallel theology exists. But the Latin American would not typically choose to conceptualize an action in terms of sin and guilt; his emphasis is on *shame*. A person is censured as being *sin verguenza*, i.e., with no sense of shame. There are variations on the expression: "He does not know how to be ashamed." "I feel shame." "What a shameful act." The difference is that one's behavior is judged relative to the standards of the group, the individual's honor within his group, and the group's honor—the family name, or the national honor. This ethical system is strongest when the individual is conscious that the group's eyes are on him; it is less an internalized self-censure. Thus failure at a task, such as an examination or even a sports event, tends to bring on feelings that are equivalent in emotional response to the feelings Americans experience following actions which Americans might consider morally wrong. Inter-American schools in military technology encounter a serious dilemma in failing a student, for a Latin American student feels more strongly that he has failed his group than would an Anglo-Saxon, who is given more leeway to flunk on his own account. It is harder for such a student to return home. (A few years ago a Brazilian soccer team had to be returned home at night on an unannounced schedule to avoid hostile crowds after they had lost out in the international soccer matches.)

This is not to say that the Latin American does not feel some religious or divine pressure for moral behavior. But he sees this aspect more mystically, and less surely directed toward specific actions. And, in turn, the American may say on occasion that he "feels ashamed of himself." But the point is that the North American more typically conceptualizes his ethics in terms of a sin-guilt motif, the Latin American in terms of group obligation and responsibility for his and his group's honor. The language used is a clue to this difference in ethical rationale. Many other societies present some variation of the group-shame orientation to ethics.

The above discussion would suggest, then, that one of the main objectives in learning a foreign language might well be to gain some insight into the perception and reasoning habits of the people who speak it. To do so requires paying close attention while learning the language to the way the language conceptualizes actions and events, and to the way the native speaker chooses among alternatives in expression. We often have occasion to say "It loses something in translation." If we know what it was that was lost, we would be a step further along in understanding the thought habits behind the language. Unfortunately, when people are taught foreign languages, this aspect is rarely pointed out. For people working in foreign affairs this might be the most important part of the language course.

Total Language Structure and the Reasoning Process

Up to this point we have been concerned with language variables at the level of words and phrases. Now let us shift our attention to the possible effects of differences in the overall structure of language. Comparative study shows that languages differ considerably in the way they bring ideas and concepts together in sentences and in more extended oral or written expression. There are minor differences, such as placing some parts of German verbs at the end of the sentence, or placing the adjective after the noun in French. In some exotic languages word ideas function so differently that they cannot be defined as nouns or verbs, for example. And the way in which sentences—if one can call them that—interrelate elements of action and description is not at all comparable with sentence structure in Indo-European languages. Can it be that the problem of translation goes beyond the translatability of words and phrases to a deeper problem of translating the inner logic of a language? Does the relationship between language and perception necessarily include the very framework of the language, which controls how ideas are strung together and interconnected? If language is fundamental to human reasoning, are cognitive processes patterned differently by different language structures, in that the language supplies the individual with a series of unconscious assumptions as to how the elements of his experiences and perceptions are related to each other? If so, the relevance to foreign affairs and public diplomacy would be highly important.

An analogy might make this line of reasoning more understandable. In modern social science it is fashionable to construct *models* as heuristic devices for investigating relationships among parts of social, economic, or political systems. They are especially important when the computer is to be used in analysis. With a hypothetical model one proposes a framework of manageable categories of phenomena to be investigated, and suggests a probable set of significant interrelationships. One might even make diagrams showing the interrelationships among members of a group (sociograms), of the power structure of an organization, or of a set of interacting economic factors. A model has the great advantage of giving some structure to the selection of data, so that the researcher does not accumulate a random collection of observations. It has the disadvantage, of course, of possibly ruling out certain observations or kinds of data which might be significant. But practically, one cannot explore all the possible interconnections of, let us say, stock prices, productivity, interest rates, and balance of trade. However, if the problem is reduced to specific factors, such as one particular stock price index and a GNP index, the study will be more manageable. The model might show that the connection between interest rates and stock prices is the primary interrelationship, and lines might be drawn to indicate the way the other factors relate to the problem.

A language, then, is something of a "model" for conceptualizing the pattern of interrelationships among the multitude of data in the physical and social world. Like any model, it preconditions the observer to perceive some relationships as more important than others, and it serves as a ready-made guide for analyzing the selected data. That is, language becomes a model for reasoning.

This aspect of comparative linguistics is in its infancy. Anthropologists and linguistic scientists have, with some trepidation, moved in close enough to discover this field and name it. They call it "metalinguistics." But they have not followed it through to the depth it deserves. There is now a somewhat related field of psycholinguistics, but much of its work has been done within single language systems, and it has concentrated on the relationships between differing emotional states or social conditions and linguistic patterns. This work is not directly applicable to foreign affairs problems. Philosophers and philologists have occasionally concerned themselves with language and conceptualization as part of their interest in comparative philosophy as seen in language and literature. Perhaps the most pertinent exploration has been made by thoughtful translators and interpreters.[16] Less systematically, diplomats and other foreign affairs specialists with long experience in exotic language areas have interested themselves in the subject.

Consequently, this discussion is pursued in a somewhat tentative way. It is intended more to draw attention to this as yet vague aspect of language analysis than to try to achieve any definitive exposition. It rests on a conviction, however, that if there is any significant substance in this dimension of language analysis, it would be of the greatest importance in understanding international communication processes.

The English language is a subject-predicate "model," as are most of the Indo-European languages. The subject-predicate quality leads one to look for a fixed descriptive relationship between subjects or things and their qualities or attributes (e.g., the lake *is* blue; the stove *is* hot). Thus English tends to suggest, as Aristotelian logic does, that something *is* or *is not;* it is good or bad, black or white. It takes much more effort to describe conditions which are not exactly one way or another—a problem which modern scientists face when they use English to discuss molecular motion or relativity. In its conception of action and events, English is an actor-action-result model, and tends to suggest this perception of the universe and what happens in it. The actor-action-result pattern is very useful for conceptualizing mechanics, business, and much of science. It suggests the question "What *caused* that?" or "What effect will this have on the end result?" This pattern is consistent with the American personality pattern, and with the optimistic and activistic outlook which seems to underlie the success achieved by English-speaking societies in their highly productive, scientific economic system.

Chinese is a substantially different model although it also provides for a subject-verb-object sequence. However, rather than implying a yes-or-no approach, or an is-or-is not quality, or a polarity in an either-or conceptualization, it emphasizes more reciprocal and complementary ordering of relationships. Black and white become two ends of a continuum which is mostly some shade of gray. One does not exist without the other. Love and hate, man and woman, hardness and softness—such qualities do not appear to represent discrete entities. One does not have to choose one *or* the other as one perceives the surrounding universe. Such qualities are only the mutually related ends of a scale; one fixes attention on the quality of the scale or continuum, not on the two ends. Stuart Chase wonders how the Chinese adjust for Marxism in China, particularly for the masses, for Communism as put together by Marx and Lenin appears to be more rigidly bipolar.[17]

If the English language structure is so congenial to the thought processes which go with science, management skills, business operations, and the like, is it possible that people using languages less tuned to this kind of thinking are at a disadvantage in coping with the modern science-oriented world? For example, Malay, Indonesian, and especially some of the related languages spread through the island area into the Philippines seem to provide weak structures for handling complicated cause and effect relationships. People in this area who do engage in abstract thinking to run businesses or manage technical operations typically deal with their subjects in some Indo-European language or in Chinese. This raises the question whether genuine self-sustaining economic development may not require, along with capital, tools, skills, and all the rest, a switch to a language more suitable for the kind of thinking which necessarily goes with modern technology. If so, then the movement for national languages in these areas might not be consistent with the desire for modernization.

There is a temptation to scale languages from primitive to modern in terms of the degree to which they lend themselves to abstract thinking, and to define as primitive those that confine the user to the concrete treatment of that which is immediately observable or tangible in feeling and emotion. There is some evidence to support such scaling, but the conclusion is far from certain. Perhaps it is useful to note that children increase their ability to use abstractions as they mature into adult roles and concerns. The key consideration probably is not just the ability to engage in abstract thought itself, but the ability to manipulate ideas and concepts abstractly in organized ways toward results which can be brought back to bear on more concrete problems. For this facility, languages do seem to offer varying degrees of support.[18]

In foreign affairs we are primarily interested in relatively abstract communication. In this regard we have a threefold problem: how well a language lends itself to handling abstract perception and reasoning in the first place; how the language structure tends to program such processes; and how people, by cultural conditioning, habitually approach logic and reasoning. On the last point, for example, in debate and in analysis we differentiate between a deductive and an inductive reasoning process. In the deductive mode we start with accepted general principles and work our way to conclusions on the supposition that if our principles and logic are correct, empirical evidence will substantiate the conclusion. With this approach, it is intellectually acceptable to conduct a course in university physics without using a laboratory, a standard procedure in many places. In the inductive approach we start with the evidence, that which we can test and be sure of, and work our way to general principles.

Bryant Wedge and Edmund Glenn have compared the typical thinking about political subjects which they observed among students in the United States, Russia, France, and the Dominican Republic.[19] For analysis purposes, Wedge and Glenn chose two kinds of differentiation in cognition styles by which the students perceived and reasoned about national and international issues. One was their intellectual use of evidence and information in acquiring knowledge and belief. At one end of this scale they placed association—a relatively uncomplicated form of incorporating new knowledge and belief; at the other they placed rational thinking and abstract reasoning. The second differentiation was the style of logic and reasoning used. This continuum ranged from a very deductive pattern, which started with broad and "universal" principles, to a very inductive pattern, which stressed attention to presented evidence and was "case particular" in application. They found that typical national student styles tended to emerge. Brazilian students tended to acquire new knowledge and belief through an association process which easily resulted in fixed universalistic persuasions. From this point on their logic patterns were essentially deductive. To convince them of a new conclusion required associating the new knowledge in their minds with respected authorities or with existing belief. Their reasoning would then tend to follow without much regard for evidence. American students, on the other hand, tended more to acquire new knowledge and belief through a rational and abstractive process. They then reached their conclusions on a case-by-case basis—not applying a universal set of assumptions—and tended to be inductive in their logic and reasoning. The Russian students were like the Americans in the way they acquired knowledge and belief, but were universalistic and deductive in logic and subsequent reasoning. This model is experimental, and the experimental evidence is fragmentary, hence the authors advise caution in using this still somewhat hypothetical analytical technique. Still, they are satisfied that such differences in cognitive processes do exist, and Glenn especially believes that such differences are associated with language.

For example, he has been interested in some studies of official translations of debates in the United Nations which tried to identify the differences in logical and analytical approaches which seem typical in the languages used, and the effects which such differences had on optimum communication.[20] American patterns tended to be inductive, with careful examination of the facts and figures and an interest in verifying the data and checking with actual experience before proceeding to more general principles. The Russian and the French styles turned more to the deductive, calling for agreement on the general principle, from which the details would fall in line. The Russians typically went to great lengths to categorize issues in debate, such as branding an action "imperialism" or an item as a political rather than an economic problem; once the category of issue was decided, the conclusions would be drawn more or less automatically. (It was interesting to note that Indians, although using English, tended toward the Russian/French pattern.)

Such studies are far from conclusive, and contrasts in approach to debate often are more a matter of degree than of sharp distinction. However, it is evident, especially to interpreters, that this kind of confusion constantly affects communication even in such an enlightened international forum as the United Nations, and that it is exceedingly difficult to arrive at translations which can carry the full intended meaning, implication, and nuance of the original. When translations are prepared for mass audiences, the difficulty is compounded.

Prestige Systems among Languages

One further facet of the effect which using one language versus another has on effective meaning is the differing attitudes and feelings which are held for the various languages themselves. In a given situation, the use of one language rather than another usually has social meaning. Through much of modern history, the French language and the ability to speak it carried an aura of prestige in the international community. The stature of an international exchange, perhaps even its validity, was enhanced by a French-language text of the proceedings. It provided an accepted common denominator or authoritative reference for exact meaning. This practice is changing, but it probably served an important function. Now that English has become a predominant world language, there tend to be subtle differences in prestige between the various varieties of English, with a proper British accent still holding an edge in many places. In fact, a few years ago there was something of a fad for bringing British secretaries to work in American business offices—the accent added a prestigious tone on the telephone and at the reception desk.

At the United Nations one frequently finds behind-the-scenes maneuvering regarding precedence among the "official" languages used in debate and in translation of the reams of documents which flow from that organization. English, French, Spanish, and Russian enjoy a certain self-assurance. Chinese is more hard pressed to justify itself. When addressing the General Assembly or its committees, a speaker from a country with a less cosmopolitan language has to choose between using his native language as a demonstration of national pride, or an accepted world language to prove his erudition—and assure communication.

A situation with the greatest potential for attitudinal strain is one which involves the subtle association of a language with the degree of civilization of the group which uses it. In areas where a non-Western language is the popular language of the people, and therefore their bond of national identity, facility in a Western language is often the mark of education and social importance—such as speaking French in Southeast Asia and parts of Africa, or English in India, Africa, or the Philippines (American English). Dutch used to be the language of social strivers in Indonesia. To a certain extent, English connotes prestige in Latin America, even though it is reluctantly granted by some. The problem of social attitudes toward a language becomes apparent when a choice has to be made as to which language should be used, and by whom, when some degree of bilingualism is involved. It can be a problem even among the nationals of one country. The late President René Barrientos of Bolivia gained considerable political strength by his ability to carry his ideas directly to his peasant electorate in Quechua. But he always made it clear that he was fluent in Spanish so that the peasants would know that he was competent to defend their interests at the national level. On the other side of the coin, the urban elites were suspicious of his Quechua, for it seemed to them to be too much of an identification with what they considered the lower and less prestigious part of the national society. In Africa, India and Pakistan, and similar areas where local language differences are associated with strong local loyalties—one can trust a member of one's own language community, but not a member of another—national level politicians have even more complicated problems.[21]

In these situations the foreigner is in trouble whatever he does. If the local language is difficult and he can conduct his important business with bilingual local people, he probably will learn only enough of the local language to give instructions to cooks and gardeners who are not bilingual. This may be considered aloofness by the local nationals, with the added negative implication of pretentious cultural superiority. It is similar to the attitude of a French-speaking grandmother in New Orleans who held until the day she died that "If anyone has anything important to say, he can say it in French."

On the other hand, the well-meaning but fumbling attempt to

use a local non-Western language may signal more condescension than empathy, especially in places where use of the local language is not absolutely necessary. In an editorial in an English-language newspaper in Manila,[22] Carmen Guerrero Nakpil, an articulate advocate for an enlightened Philippine nationalism and increased sense of national identity, complained that because of points made in the then recent book *The Ugly American,* resident Americans were taking crash courses in Tagalog, and that one ranking official's wife had rocked the women's club circuit by making (probably reading) a speech in Tagalog. She pointed out that Filipinos were not very favorably impressed by such efforts, that they were either amused or offended when a foreigner tried to talk Tagalog to them. They suspected that it was a joke, or that they were being talked down to, especially when the listener was more fluent in English than the foreigner was in Tagalog. She concluded that considering the improbability that the foreigner would actually become fluent in Tagalog, "It seems a waste to take so much trouble just to be misunderstood."

It should not necessarily be concluded that attempts to learn difficult local languages should be abandoned—quite the contrary. The potential for effective international communication is clearly greater with than without knowledge of the language. But there are significant connotations simply in *who* uses a language, and why; the intent in using a language is communicated as surely as the message itself. It is important to recognize that a little bit of learning in a local language is probably more rewarding when the effort is directed toward understanding how that language structures the thought processes and perception patterns of the people who use it, than when the effort is directed only toward an immediate translation facility. This facet of language learning is grossly neglected.

VI

From Patterns of

Thinking to the

Behavior of Nations

THE TITLE OF THIS CHAPTER SUGGESTS A LONG STEP. Yet it is a direct, and in fact, a logical one. Any behavior, be it individual or collective, as in the case of a nation, rests on some combination of assumptions and desired objectives, whether they are coldly and rationally calculated, or merely reflect the conventional wisdom of the society and result from an irrational and unconscious interplay of emotional and attitudinal predispositions. Clearly there is an association between the culture and national experience of a people and the pattern of values, assumptions, and attitudes which they inject into their approach to foreign relations. As today's international relations are carried out more and more in the arena of public diplomacy, collective participation insures the connection between popular patterns of thinking and the nation's international behavior. Therefore, we come to understand that such factors as a nation's style in conducting international relations, its objectives, its conception of what international circumstances are tolerable or intolerable, and its preferences for one kind of solution or accommodation over another are extensions of the particular patterns of perception and reasoning which can be expected to be different in every nation.

If there were no distinctive national traits, no nationalism, and no real difference in outlook or objective among nations, most of the more difficult problems in international affairs would disappear. The Middle East problem would lose its quality of explosive intransigence; there would be no ideological confrontation between East and West; deliberations in the United Nations would sound more like those in a state legislature. Only an ethnocentric simpleton would venture into international diplomacy believing that because all men are brothers they will think alike and that all nations will respond with the same perception and logic.

It might be argued that the effects of mass psychology are greatly diminished because a nation's policy makers and diplomats are, after all, objective and urbane people, quite able to understand one another, that the conventional ways of handling international problems have been around for a long time, and that members of foreign affairs communities in general share a kind of international understanding of issues and a certain rationality which reduces the cross-cultural psychological dimension to a factor of little consequence. But this argument is false on two counts.

In the first place, the men and women who participate in decision making and negotiation are still human, despite their socialization in the rarified atmosphere of international diplomacy and the rational calculation which is expected of them in their jobs. Consciously or not, they share to some degree the emotions and outlooks of their society, and a personal identification with the interests of the public they represent. Their "definition of the situation" reflects this fact. Few completely impartial brokers exist in the international negotiation business, and they probably would not be trusted to represent a country in any case. Further, as human beings, their individual personalities always enter into the style and process of decision making and negotiating, and individual personality is always relative to some cultural base. In

The Psychological Dimension of Foreign Policy,[1] Joseph H. de Rivera discusses at length the way in which individual personality and perception have entered into significant foreign policy decisions in the United States, particularly decisions during the Korean War. One of the interesting implications of this study is the degree to which decision makers, for all their intended objectivity, are nevertheless often unconsciously bound to both personalized and society-based perceptions of international issues. The book also documents the way in which their image of their position in government and of their role expectations play a part in their view of the issues and the response required.

Secondly, as stated in preceding chapters, in this day of intensive communication and increasing public participation in foreign affairs issues, the policy maker's options are relatively limited to those decisions which make some sense to the involved public. Decisions must respond to popular perceptions of the issues and popular objectives. Both decision and tactic have to fit reasonably well into the public's tolerable limits of morality, or of national pride. These limits differ markedly, of course, from one society to another, and the tactics and objectives of foreign policy leaders vary accordingly, even though they may personally prefer to adhere to the conventions of international negotiation and problem solving.

The fact that few policies in any country are the creations of a single individual tends to insure that the conventional wisdom of the group is injected into the choice of decision and tactic. At the least a staff processes pertinent information and provides interpretations of it, thus multiplying the number of personalities reflecting the perceptions and logic of the society in reaching a decision. At the upper end of the scale of group involvement within governmental processes, a congress or parliament may engage in extended debate on an issue before a decision is made, or on ratifying an agreement afterward. When it comes to policy execution, the perception and reasoning patterns of the group continue to affect the national behavior, for whether an army or an

Embassy is charged with doing it, the execution is carried out by groups of men. They reinforce each other in the "common sense" of their society as they determine the style in which the policy is to be executed, and the adaptations and adjustments which have to be made in the actual application. In turn, those in the field report back on the policy's fortunes, and give their view of situations requiring further decisions. Again the interpretation will encounter the subjective subtleties of group dynamics, and the rational and objective purity of the decision-making process yields further to a group-reinforced input from the larger society's informal assumptions and understanding. For better or for worse, this group wisdom is most assured in democratic societies, and in governments in which the committee and the interagency group approach is taken in reaching a judgment of the issues and finally a decision. Thus the connection between a nation's behavior and its underlying thought processes is reinforced.

The Place of Values in a Realistic Theory of International Relations

The effect which value orientations and public patterns of reasoning have on the behavior of nations, and the effect they *should* have, have been the subject of much debate in the theory of international relations. In the 1950s the American foreign affairs community followed with particular interest the arguments of George Kennan and Hans Morgenthau, who, in effect, counseled that the society's moral and legal persuasions and its public opinion of the moment should not be allowed to distract the policy maker from the more realistic appreciation of the nation's interests and the realities of the relationships between national powers. Kennan suggested that perhaps the United States had exaggerated the role of such matters as moral and legal principles as determinants of its foreign policy; that in the long run this created more difficulties and even more conflict in the international arena, and did not allow for objective calculation of the country's own national interest in setting its course of action. He argued that diplomacy should be delegated to an ever more competent professionalized corps of diplomatic specialists who would provide the lead for taking actions more clearly in the national interest and less subject to emotionalism or to "diplomacy by dilettantism"—his term for too many inexperienced people getting into the act. He suggested that the role of moral principle was to strengthen the quality of American society to provide a better basis for international leadership.[2]

Hans Morgenthau was associated even more with the idea that an appreciation of reality must come first in choosing the course of foreign policy; morality would too easily cloud the issue. He stressed that nations have their interests, and in the absence of a controlling international society to protect these interests and to maintain a balance in a community of nations, "reality" must come first. A nation would thus pursue the interests of its own people—morally if possible, but objectively in any case.[3]

However, in this age of public diplomacy, when subjective outlooks of the various sectors of American society—and of other societies as well—tend to press more articulately and insistently on the policy-decision process, there is a real question whether Kennan's and Morgenthau's call for such a detached objectivity is itself fully "realistic." It is more probable that the moral persuasion and the subjective attitude embodied in public opinion will come to affect policy more, rather than less. Actually, political scientists in recent years have argued that there is something artificial in analyzing international relations decisions with a conceptual model which assumes that nations can act as monolithic units in choosing their policies rationally or "realistically." They note that even before the public's definition of the situation exerts itself, there are several levels of interplay within a modern government by which decisions can turn out to be the results of organizational and bureaucratic processes themselves. The various components of government must resolve their views of the objective as seen from their differing positions of responsibility— the diplomats, the generals, the budget men and the lawmakers all may have an input, even in a crisis. Bureaucratic politics inject considerations that are often far removed from the central issue as the actors in the decision-making process compete and bargain for intramural advantage.[4]

As the debate of the 1950s drew more attention, the late Frank Tannenbaum went to considerable lengths to present a counter argument in his book *The American Tradition in Foreign Policy*.[5] He developed the case that Americans do have a unique point of view regarding society and government, which has been extended into their international relations for many years, and that when policy has ignored this point of view or has been inconsistent with it, the policy has created dissension at home, has lacked full cooperation, and has usually been ineffective. He stressed especially that Americans have a historic belief in the "co-ordinate state," that is, a belief in the sovereign integrity and equality of each state—a logical extension of their guiding belief in the individual and in equality among states in the national society. This belief was the basis of American federalism. Extended into international relations, it rejects balance-of-power arrangements or overbearing control by more powerful nations over less powerful ones, whether such arrangements are in the "realistic" national interest of the dominant nations or not. The co-ordinate state outlook would have all nations live free of coercion, and free to exercise their will in their own affairs and in their own internal interests. Any system of international control and regulation among nations would be bound to observe this principle.

Tannenbaum observed that this principle has its roots in the national experience and in the associated value orientations of American life: value placed on the individual, sympathy for the weak and the underdog, the pursuit of one's own destiny, the idea that all men are created equal, that ordinary folk count. The outlook was consistent with the melting-pot development of

American society, and the comparatively high degree of racial, cultural, and religious tolerance which resulted. American national experience also led to the assumption that cooperative action is the preferred way to resolve problems, preferably by local determination, dealing with issues as they arise. Rejecting a hierarchical concept of society, Americans also have rejected a hierarchical system among nations. They see democracy essentially as a way of government rather than simply a theory of government, and tend to deal accordingly among nations.

Thus in Tannenbaum's development, the collective mental set supporting the American outlook on the co-ordinate state also explains the American approach to such foreign affairs positions as the Open Door policy in the Far East, the Good Neighbor policy in Latin America, Wilson's Fourteen Points, intervention in Korea, etc. It was this outlook which made the take-over of the Philippines such a dilemma for Americans, for a purely imperialistic control was felt to be inconsistent with the inner American logic in foreign affairs. At the least Americans had to persuade themselves that they had assumed a responsibility to prepare the Filipinos for independence—that this was the purpose of going forward with administration of the islands.

Samples of characteristic international behavior resulting from particular configurations of assumptions and perceptions abound; a case study could be made of any nation.

African nations present a pattern of preoccupations in international affairs which has been loosely associated with "negritude," that is, a memory of colonial experience combined with a certain consciousness of racial and cultural distinctiveness, which seems to generate strong feelings of hostility and aggressiveness in dealing with non-African countries. It is a mood, or an attitudinal predisposition, which is often evident regardless of the specific issue, or the degree of common interest otherwise present.[6]

Among the many outlooks and assumptions which explain Latin American international behavior is the preoccupation with personal and national honor, which has been built into a high sensitivity to national boundary issues. It has reached the level that the very selection of a site for an Inter-American conference is plagued with the problem of finding neutral ground, and delegates often attend on the condition that they will have an opportunity to speak about their country's boundary concerns, regardless of the purpose of the conference. Many of the disputes took place many years ago, but the priority attention given to them makes the perceptions involved salient determinants of international behavior.

Switzerland expects to play a unique role in international affairs as it carries its self-image of the neutral and honest broker for central Europe. Swiss policy, and thus its international behavior, derive from this special Swiss view of itself, and of the world.

One of the strong motivations in Japanese postwar international activity has been a real concern for Japan's international image following the collapse of its wartime adventure and the resentments engendered in the process. It seems to have supplied part of the inspiration for the extraordinary energy the Japanese have expended in their domestic reconstruction—the world was watching their response to defeat. And it seems to have prompted a high degree of cooperation in international development programs in the years since.

Whatever the subject in international debate in recent years, the Arab countries have tended to state the issues in terms of a near obsession with their conflict with Israel. But their preoccupation involves much more than the antagonisms of ethnic incompatibility, conflict for territory, or even the sting of defeat. The psychological roots go down through many generations. Their beliefs and attitudes are so deeply embedded in the personality structure that change by any rational argument, no matter how skillfully presented, is precluded. The perceptions involved are not just political or economic in nature, or simply matters of national pride. They are deeply moral and religious; they involve a holy war.

How a nation conceives of its nationalism is an important cognitive orientation for its international behavior. Edmund Glenn has called attention to two differing conceptions of national identity. One involves a loyalty to, and identity with, the population living within the boundaries of a national state, and a sense of cohesiveness as a result of common experience and mutual interest. The United States, Canada, or England would display a nationalism of this kind. The other is an ethnic and linguistic identity, a special sense of belonging to one's ethnic group wherever one goes, regardless of nation-state boundaries. Many of the nationalistic antagonisms of Central and Eastern Europe reflect this conception; German nationalism has been a specific example. Jewish nationalism, and even pan-Africanism, carry this conception. International behavior, as a function of nationalistic sentiments, varies accordingly.[7]

Observers in areas of French colonial influence note that a certain complex of French value orientations which seems to equate French Culture (with a capital "C") with civilization has traveled with French administrations. Here is a case in which a self-image has established a special international identity which makes a subtle impact on the French approach to international affairs. If countries had trademarks French Culture would be the French insignia.

Yet, however a nation chooses its own policy, it tends to assume cold calculation on the part of other nations. Some observers note that with France's status as a great power being challenged, the French must view the recent polarization of world politics with misgivings. They prefer to see the contest as multiple, for neither their self-image nor their long view of the future tolerates their relegation to a satellite position *vis-à-vis* one or the other of the two camps. Historical experience has tinged the French outlook with the cynicism of lost innocence. The French expect large powers to behave in a way that preserves their privileged position, and they find unconvincing the American insistence that its use of power is identical with the interests of mankind. This attitude of selfless superiority is rejected as moralistic window dressing, used by a nation which is naive, inexperienced, and somewhat drunk on its own power.[8]

Although Kennan, Morgenthau, and Tannenbaum were singled out, many writers in international relations have taken up the discussion of national motivation.[9] The issue has never been whether value orientations and philosophical persuasions *are* injected into the choice of a nation's policy, but how far a nation can pursue its moral preferences and how much it must concede to some degree of *realpolitik*. But the point to be recognized is that reasonably objective scientific study of human society and culture indicates that whether or not philosophical or less than rational factors *should* determine the behavior of nations, the fact is they will. Moral systems and value orientations, basic assumptions popularly held, beliefs and knowledge whether distorted or not, attitudes and prejudices will in some degree be reflected in the collective behavior of a nation. Policies which call on a nation to play a part which is out of character are usually not persuasive in the international arena, and lack support at home. So-called objective and realistic policy deliberations must take this fact into account if they are *actually to be objective and realistic*.

Even in the Soviet Union or Communist China, where forceful and comprehensive changes of government have been specifically designed to implant new systems of reasoning and logic in government, existing assumptions and beliefs persist, and a Russian or Chinese foreign policy is not entirely an intellectual abstraction. It does not immediately cast Russians or Chinese completely out of character. The qualified foreign affairs expert still needs a good knowledge of Russian history and a good understanding of traditional Russian fears and prejudices, or of Chinese thought and culture.

Public diplomacy, then, makes its impact on the traditional theory and practice of international relations by its insistence that the whole complex of psychological and philosophical factors be specifically included in any analysis of the international behavior of nations. It also suggests that any analysis which leaves out this complex and derives its conclusions regarding a nation's intentions only by assuming a rational and *realpolitik* design behind the action runs a severe risk of misunderstanding motives and objectives. Once one takes a purposeful approach in coping with this "softer" dimension, the main factors turn out to be less mysterious, irrational, and unpredictable than they may appear at first. The approach may be along two lines. On the one hand are the formal beliefs and value orientations directly relevant to a given government and to its actions. On the other are the less obvious psychocultural factors which lead to the choice and style of response. For the United States let us briefly review first the more direct and formal orientations, and then the less formal and less recognized factors which help mold our American style in foreign affairs. Following that, let us compare the case of the Soviet Union.

The American Logic in Governmental and Foreign Affairs

It is interesting to note that Frederick H. Hartmann, in his book *The New Age of American Foreign Policy*,[10] chose to devote two introductory chapters to an examination of the way in which a characteristic pattern of American outlook has carried over into a typically American approach to problems in foreign affairs. The chapter titles are "The Unusualness of American Experience" and "The Impact of American Attitudes." He uses this review to emphasize that there is a uniquely American rationale both in the way our foreign policy apparatus is organized and in the decisions reached. He points out that this outlook went through its formative state in geographical isolation during most of our first century of independence, during which a self-assurance was developed in meeting the domestic challenges of the new environment and the frontier. Cultural mixture presented problems in achieving consensus, but these problems were resolved through free debate and compromise. Idealism gave purpose to early national experience; pragmatism made the evolving system work. Such domestic experience helped precondition American expectations for meeting international problems.

More specifically, Hartmann reminds his readers that the key to the American approach to governmental and political problems is seen in the contractual conception of government found, among other places, in the constitution. Note how some of the related idea patterns regarding government could affect the way of looking at foreign affairs. Government is seen as an institution which provides the mechanisms and the procedural skills for executing policies and programs while the public sits in the driver's seat to decide which actions and policies should be delegated to the government machinery. To insure this arrangement the constitution pays careful attention to balancing the powers of government and to reserving specific rights to the states and to individual citizens. The thought pattern behind this is a *problem-solving orientation* to government. The constitution and subsequent laws have established the ground rules and the *methods* for reaching decisions and for checking over their execution. This is the revered and idealistic aspect of the American system of government—the "government of laws and not of men." But the system leaves the *content* of the solution of problems to men. Thus government fits the pragmatic approach which has come to be the American preference in meeting collective problems.

This combination of an ideal method and a problem-solving pragmatism for resolving problems has carried over into American assumptions in international relations. It is seen particularly clearly in the United Nations. It explains the high expectation that the U.N. is a *way* to carry out the *pragmatic resolution* of international problems—and the sense of frustration when other nations approach the United Nations with differing objectives and concepts of its function.

Hartmann also noted that the American experience is reflected in the American preference today for direct action by government in meeting and solving international problems. This does not appear to be consistent with the original idea that government should be the servant waiting for its master's orders. This revised view followed a change in the American concept of the proper scope of action for the federal government. After national life became so complicated that many of the nation's problems could be met only at the national level, positive action by government was the logical recourse—albeit granted with reluctance by those who cherished the highest degree of local control. As national security became more of a concern by the beginning of the twentieth century, it also called for national-level purposive action. By the end of World War II, a predisposition for positive action in the international arena was advanced even further. Thus in foreign affairs Americans tended not only to inject themselves and their government into resolution of the broad range of postwar international problems but to do so with a strong bent for getting the job done forthwith. With a relatively weak sense of history and a tendency to think in terms of the present and the future rather than the past, with a tendency to take positions quickly, and with an optimistic confidence that all problems had solutions, the American thrust assumed a unique quality, which was an asset when action and leadership were required. But it was a source of frustration when dealing with nations with other perspectives of time and history, and with less assurance that positive and direct action necessarily would be the best way. The end result in foreign policy is that Americans tend to be strongly optimistic but lacking in patience; they tend to underestimate the tenacity of the problem; and may tend to assume larger roles than they can ultimately fulfil.

Another source for contrasting ideas about government, which in turn affects perceptions in international issues, is found in the thought patterns implicit in the contractual relationship between the individual and government. John Locke's principle was that all social life and government should have their foundations in the dignity, liberty, and happiness of the individual. This conception of "natural rights"—the idea of a ring of immunity and privacy surrounding the individual—became an integrating rationale for American-style democratic government and for its actions. Government became a moral trust dependent on the free consent of the governed. These background assumptions, then, also became part of the American's cognitive mold for perceiving and reasoning about government's role in international affairs.

This orientation is not universal, and the American viewpoint becomes clearer when compared to other societies in which existing patterns of social relations place primary emphasis on the group or the society itself, rather than on the individual, and the worth and meaning of the individual are defined in terms of the larger collectivity and its well-being. Most traditional societies tend to shift the emphasis in this direction, that is from the individual to the group, from individualism to group identity. These are quite different views. When internalized in "national character," they serve to predispose members of the two kinds of society to perceive governmental issues differently, a difference which has complicated communication and debate in the international arena.

Stephen Rhinesmith reviewed the debate which took place in the United Nations when a draft Declaration of Human Rights was being considered in the early years of the U.N. (1946–48).[11] He studied especially the contrasting American and Russian conceptions of "human rights," and the effect they had on agreeing on a text. (There was agreement that a declaration *should* be formulated.) The Americans, led by Mrs. Eleanor Roosevelt, clearly started with the assumption that human rights were individualized in nature, pertained to the person, and were innate and inviolable. The Russian delegation started just as clearly with the contrasting assumption that "rights" did not exist unless they were defined and insured by the collectivity, and when it was in the society's interest, they were extended to the individual. Further, the Americans saw "rights" as being essentially political; the Russians had a more comprehensive conception, and urged a longer list including "rights" to work, to old-age security, leisure, education, maternity care. Also, the Russians seemed to associate rights more directly with the citizen's duties to the collectivity, while the Americans were less specific on this manner. The debate did not end in agreement between the Americans and the Russians, but in a committee conclusion in which the Russians were outvoted. In the final vote the Russians abstained as the adopted wording leaned toward the American point of view.

The same pattern of perceptions can complicate communication at a less formal level. A visiting Russian professor of journalism recently presented a guest lecture before a group of American graduate students. In the question and answer session afterward the discussion centered on the responsibility of the press in reporting the news. Specifically, the question was whether it would be in the "public interest" for the press to refrain from reporting events in full detail when it might be injurious to the larger society's well-being (the larger society being represented by government). The students argued that it is basically in the public interest to report facts as fully and correctly as possible. The guest took the opposing view, and further stated that the purpose of public information is to form attitudes which support the public interest. The students felt the purpose is to inform. Even allowing for some linguistic difficulties, it was clear that the real question was the conception of "public interest," and of who should decide what the interest is. The Soviet visitor assumed that the press has its first obligation to the collectivity, whether he was conscious of that assumption in the moment of debate or not. According to the American students, the responsibility of the press is to the people who make up the public itself so that being informed, *they* can decide what their public interest is.

A similar kind of divergence in underlying assumptions affects the perception of issues when democratic institutions and practices are discussed internationally. The American concept of democracy started out essentially as a political concept, with emphasis on equality under law and justice, and on equality in participation in the political process. Freedom was a central theme, particularly freedom from political domination and arbitrary authority. The right to hold private property and freedom to exercise individual initiative to individual advantage in a capitalistic system were consistent with, and indeed part of, the American concept of democracy. However, many societies with differing social structures and economic concerns focused more on competing for limited resources than on conquering a frontier; equality in an economic sense came to be as important, or even more important, than freedom and equality in a political sense. Freedom from unemployment, from labor exploitation, and from structured poverty were salient preoccupations. Equal opportunity and access to resources, and even equality in income, held an appeal in such societies. Thus, to the dismay of Americans, socialism at the least, and even Communism, laid claim to the "democracy" title. The result has been widespread confusion in international communication both at the official level and in ideological propaganda and public information programs. The basis for confusion involves differing concerns and priorities as to what the individual should be "free" from, in what sense people should be "equal," and in the relevance of these matters to the political process.

One of the very real problems in United States foreign policy deliberations is that the American public not only naturally takes a highly ethnocentric view toward the various theories and forms of government around the world but also tends toward a kind of selective perception which focuses disproportionally on *forms* and procedures, especially when some pretension to democratic government is involved. Thus Americans use the popular vote as a standard for evaluating other governments, regardless of whether such factors as the degree of literacy or of informed opinion, or the degree to which a system allows manipulation of voting blocs by narrow interests might negate the intended function of voting. If the people vote, it is reasoned, the country is a democracy, regardless of the choice offered or the responsiveness of the resulting government to public participation. Compared to other nations, the American public has also made an unusually close cognitive association between democracy and capitalistic institutions and free enterprise. But it has resisted associating ideas of social welfare or state control of production or distribution of goods with democracy, even when such a governmental role is supported by a well-informed and free electorate, and despite the degree to which these functions have been accepted on the same popular basis in the U.S.

From a psychological point of view, this tendency to perceive and highlight form and process before substance is understandable enough. Form and institutional structure are more easily discerned in a foreign system. Substance, meaning, and function of institutions are much less concrete, and few people have a clear idea of these underlying strata of governmental theory and their practical significance. The perception problem involved reveals itself in the American public's misunderstanding of foreign governments—we err both in lauding and in downgrading other governmental practices, even by our own deeper standards, and policy makers accordingly find their range of options affected. At the same time, other foreign publics have difficulty in interpreting our intentions when they find us overinsistent—as they see it—on popular elections or on free enterprise institutions.

The American national experience has tended to make us unusually ethnocentric. We assume that our solutions to governmental problems are the universal ones, that American institutions and practices set the standards in civic and economic affairs toward which all more "backward" countries should aspire. Historically, we have been remarkably successful, both in confronting our own problems and in our initiatives in international relations. America has been the mecca for immigrants from all parts of the world, a kind of proof of the pudding which strengthens our self-assurance in our system. The American constitution and many American governmental and economic institutions have been copied abroad, reinforcing the unconscious assumption that American models are the natural, human, and moral ones. Consequently, the neutral observer sees a missionary and proselyting approach in presenting American institutions to the rest of the world, and our sense of frustration when, in the course of international events, our intentions are misunderstood, the system is criticized, or other countries choose other courses of political and economic development. This circumstance certainly is not unique to Americans, of course. But there is much evidence that it may be accentuated in our case, and that this factor, plus the prominent place which the United States occupies in international affairs, makes understanding the psychology of American ethnocentricism essential to understanding the American role in international affairs.

A Characteristic American Style in Foreign Affairs

The *way* Americans do things in international affairs is affected not only by their distinctive combination of thought patterns related to government and the issues *per se* but also by mental habits underlying an approach to life in general. To catalogue all the traits which potentially could affect this style would be a formidable task; no one has really tried to list more than the most important. Several themes or salient value orientations do stand out among the items most often mentioned by social scientists, foreign observers, and thoughtful Americans reflecting on their experiences abroad. Some of them have been discussed in previous chapters, but should be recalled here.

The first such theme we might return to is the traditional optimistic outlook by which the individual American tends to regard the world about him and its events. He is inclined to think in terms of cause and effect, and to see himself as a "cause" of the "effect." (See also Chapters II and V.) This outlook, we have said, stands in contrast to the fatalism found in many more traditional societies, where the individual sees his world as given and its events as foreordained, as circumstances which he must accept and over which he has little control. The American's more activistic bent rests, in part, on a tradition of pride in conquering the frontier and its rigors, in attacking the impossible. He believes that everything can be mastered if enough effort, genius, and ingenuity are expended. He assumes that all problems have solutions. He sees reality as basically good, and tends to see matters in their most favorable light. He minimizes the adverse. He believes that there should be a happy ending, and most significantly, that the individual can do something to help bring it about. In this, as in other value orientations, the thought may be more honored in tradition than in constant practice, and such value orientations may change. But in comparative perspective and as seen in intercultural communication, the theme is a valid consideration.

This optimistic orientation seems to have served as a motivational springboard for many historically significant American thrusts in international affairs. The Marshall Plan stemmed from this kind of perception of the situation. The Alliance for Progress did, too, perhaps out of proportion to the actual difficulty of the problem. American optimism spurs an impatience to confront the issues, to get on with the job, to do something, to set things right. In sum, it is the positive and direct action approach. It leads, however, to the uneasy feeling among less activistically-oriented allies that precipitate action may compound the problem rather than resolve it. It precludes opting for no action, which might, in the view of some critics, sometimes lead to more desirable results. Some foreign observers suggest that the American is led to the ethnocentric assumption that if the United States does not take action, nothing will be done. Thus, in the interest of a fast resolution of a problem, the U.S. does not allow time for other forces or actors on the international stage to find a solution or accommodation which might be equally effective. As their experience has accumulated in the postwar era, Americans themselves are wondering also whether their impatience for action might not have left them overextended as "the world's policeman."

Thus there is a paradox. The same value orientation which drives the American genius also leads to a greater degree of frustration and puzzlement when the direct action policy does not produce the results expected. The Viet Nam experience may be such a case. We seek the cause of the derailment when policies fail: Who sabotaged the plan? Who erred in judgment? Who lost China? This thought pattern does not easily lend itself to accepting the notion that countervailing forces were too great or were simply not amenable to manipulation from outside. The point is not that the American outlook is, by its nature, counterproductive, but that this facet of the cognitive foundation of American life must be understood and appreciated if one is to comprehend the American approach to international problems. Indeed, it has been the dynamo for American leadership in world affairs in war and in peace, and in imaginative creation of international institutions which have done much to smooth the way for ever more complex relationships among nations. The Americans are not alone in their purposeful action orientation, although they may be its most zealous proponent.

The American concept of the individual and society, which has implications for the ideological thrust of the United States, also has implications for the American style and manner in foreign affairs. The cluster of assumptions involved includes the value of individual human life, the worth and dignity of the individual, and the belief that the individual should be allowed a self-reliant expression of his talent and energy to fulfill his own promise. Value is placed on the individual conscience, and the right to express personal belief, to protest, and to reject arbitrary authority. The cluster further includes the egalitarian persuasion and the goal of equal opportunity. Again, these value orientations do not always square with actual experience or practice on the domestic scene, but they do affect perception of issues, and particularly the style of interpersonal relationships for those Americans who deal directly with foreign people. American informality, openness, and a tendency to treat other people on an equal basis, whether this means upgrading the peon or downgrading the aristocrat, are all part of the outlook.

Among other consequences, it has tended to democratize protocol. The American Embassy, never very comfortable in pursuing what it considers artificial pomp and pretension in overdone protocol, outweighs the others in size and initiative. Benjamin Franklin had trouble because his government did not want him to wear a diplomatic uniform, and several of our early presidents took delight in instructing foreign ambassadors in Washington in the ways of democratic precedence—in fact, in no precedence at all. Legend says that President Jefferson received the first British minister assigned to Washington in unkempt informal clothes and house slippers, and subsequently ordered, on the principle of social equality, a ban on precedence of any kind at official social gatherings.[12]

In extending economic and social development assistance, the American inclination is to foster mass education over specialized and elite education and to promote individual initiative in community development. The high value on human life supplies the moral motivation for disaster relief, missionary activities, and a host of humanitarian enterprises. Sometimes it complicates foreign assistance programs by adding a series of objectives which relate more to a missionary endeavor than to a calculated development program. Even when our policy involves dispatching military forces, the American outlook on the individual is pertinent. It helps explain the unique nature of the military organization—its less rigid chain-of-command relationships, the informal self-assertion on the part of the soldier, and the soldier's style from the way he carries out his duties to the way he fraternizes with the local population.

In previous chapters we have discussed the effect of American middle-class value patterns on style and approach in foreign affairs. We have emphasized the value placed on achievement, including possible misunderstandings arising from contrasting views of American "materialism," and the unique psychological need for achievement, which leads to a special outlook on entrepreneurship and economic development. The performance of American public officials is much affected by this combination of value orientations, which derives from an open, mobile, achievement-oriented society. It supports the "public service" incentive which prompts many men to go into public life in the first place. The need to validate status continually sustains motivation and productivity. There is no necessity to repeat this entire discussion, but it would be well to recall that these components of the American cognitive structure are among the most important in preconditioning an American style, and in evaluating the style and approach of other nations in their conduct of foreign affairs.

Ethics and moral practices are the basic conditioners of style and approach. These idea patterns are based on faith and profound belief, are usually ingrained in the personality at an early age, and become deeply embedded in the emotional matrix of the personality. Great objectivity is required to override them, and with the American personalized sin-guilt approach to morality and the close association between ethical behavior and religious belief, there is a strong tendency to carry moral and ethical outlooks into dealings with foreign people. Americans are less likely to take a "live and let live" or a "cultural relativity" position; they are more inclined to perceive and judge the issues and activities of their foreign counterparts in moral and ethical terms, even in puritanical terms. In different ways, both Woodrow Wilson and John Foster Dulles approached policy decisions with a strong moral ingredient in the mix of their motives.

Hence the American is quickly outraged when agreements and commitments are not lived up to, when there is deception in public statements, when the rules of fair play are ignored, or when private property is confiscated—"stolen" is his perception.

Oppression of the weak and defenseless bothers the American in his ethical as well as his humanitarian conception.

The moral and ethical foundation affects foreign affairs in other ways: There seems to be a distinctly American hesitation in using force, despite the fact that the United States has, as occasion demanded, built up the largest concentrations of force in history, including the atomic bomb. Conscientious objection to military service has had an almost unique development in the United States, both in the number of conscientious objectors and in the fact that society has seen the need to provide legal means for objecting. Proponents of "preventive" military strikes do not receive much moral support from their society. And when military force is used, the justification includes a defense of that which is moral and right; destruction is wreaked on an "immoral" enemy, and is dispatched with a sense of administering justice or punishing evil. Again, this kind of mentality is not confined to the United States, and it is subject to change over time. But in nuance and in priority in the reasoning process, its uniqueness needs to be recognized.

American fears and anxieties also affect perception and reasoning. They, too, tend to be patterned by national and group experience, and affect style and method in foreign affairs. Fear of an enemy and suspicion of foreign intentions are obvious factors. In recent years a diffuse but all-pervading anxiety regarding "Communism"—and its supposed monolithic omnipotence—has had a strong impact on American perceptions of foreign affairs issues, even among the mass of the population, who are often unable to provide an articulate definition of the term. Whether or not these fears are accurately based, the mental set has certainly had much to do with foreign policy deliberations, and with style and approach.

Less or more subtle anxieties come to mind. Some observers believe that Americans have a unique anxiety about being liked, or at least being appreciated for their accomplishments and generosity, and that this anxiety leads to reactions which seem either undignified or at least unrealistic in the colder calculations of international relations. These observers say that the United States, although a powerful nation, apparently cannot be content with merely being respected, but requires something more emotionally satisfying to the American mentality tuned to an American style of interpersonal relations. They claim to see a difference between the American affective response in this regard and those typical of other nations.

This brief survey of American psychic predispositions, although far from complete, will serve to illustrate an analytical approach which can be made in connecting characteristic patterns of thinking and the behavior of nations. A look at comparable factors in another country further establishes the relevance of these general cognitive factors. For this we turn to the Soviet Union.

Logic and Style of the Soviet Union

Perhaps in no other case have we been so aware of the relationship between unique patterns of thinking and approach to international affairs as when dealing with the Soviet Union. Even though there is a persisting Russian heritage in foreign policy outlook which blends into the new design, we understand that most of the fundamental assumptions which the Soviets carry into the foreign affairs arena derive directly from some interpretation of Marxist-Leninist theory and analysis.

As the Soviet Union has passed a half-century in its Communist format, two generations of Russian people, and especially of a new elite, have been socialized in this logic, so that what was once an intellectual abstraction may be coming closer to a pattern of conventional wisdom in somewhat the same way that the ideas of the American founding fathers have become the habitual logic of American politicians. Still, the Soviet theory is relatively new; the central problem in Communist policy frequently is to decide on the "correct" interpretation of their theory for the circumstance at hand. The Soviets often cannot agree among themselves, or interpretation changes with changing leadership. The various Communist countries display widely differing interpretations and applications of Communist theory, and struggles for power within Communist parties often reflect their dilemma. Western observers necessarily devote priority attention to current doctrine and to the dynamics of its interpretation, as a key to understanding the Soviet stance in foreign affairs.[13]

However, certain generalizations can be made about the cognitive basis for a characteristic Soviet outlook on government and foreign affairs objectives, and especially about contrasts with patterns in the United States. There is a danger in over-generalizing, and value orientations change over time in the Soviet Union as elsewhere, but it is useful to look for a basic pattern.

As a start, let us take Tannenbaum's argument that the United States tends to follow a co-ordinate conception of relationships among nations, that is, the notion that in their essential integrity and equality states should pursue their interests in self-determination fashion. This clearly is not the Soviet view. The Soviet conception of dealing with other states is submerged in the theory of process and historical evolution toward a socialist society. Hence, rather than champion self-determination, the Soviets fix their attention on change, and on evaluating stages in the process of history—feudalism, capitalism, socialism. As the Soviets see it, they wear the mantle of leadership for the process, and history is on their side. Their national interest is to promote Communism, so their international interests coincide with their domestic objectives. From this starting point they choose their allies, define their enemies, and judge the issues. This is not to say that they never pragmatically support the national sovereignty principle, especially for nations outside the Soviet orbit. But the vested interest in the progression toward Communism within sovereign states leads to a quite different foreign policy stance from that envisioned in Tannenbaum's co-ordinate state assumptions. For example, certain types of almost blatant intervention in the political processes of another country or the support of local political forces could be engaged in without the built-in restraints which would press on the United States.[14]

The essence of the Soviet approach is a dogmatic self-assurance which comes from their conviction that their view is based on rational and objective analysis, i.e., on "science" (not to be confused with the Western conception of science as an inductive testing of hypotheses). Hence, with a Marxist-Leninist monopoly on "truth" and a conviction that other analyses are "objectively wrong," they arrive at a totally different basis for judging the fundamental rights of independent states and for interacting with them. Strain is understandably produced when other Communist states see the "objective truth" about revolution differently, as, for example, in the "words of Chairman Mao" or in the Castro variant. Resulting conflicts have a psychological nuance distinct from those with states outside the Communist club. They bring to the surface a Russian insistence on being the leader of the socialist forces, which may be motivated as much by a traditional Russian sense of manifest destiny as by Communist zeal. Observers have judged that at times this objective has taken precedence over the fortunes of Communist parties in other countries.

As in the case of the Western democracies, it is important to review the moral and ethical assumptions of the society itself in order to understand Soviet perception of international events and issues. And Russian society does present a strong traditional pattern of ethical values. Yet, these ethics are probably regarded more as relative and less as universal in application, while the Communist theory supplies its own moral basis, or perhaps better, a science of ethics. In this approach morals are based on the objective condition and on the interests and needs of the society. They therefore differ from time to time and place to place. In any case, morality is determined by what is good for, or in the interest of, development of the *society*, not the individual member. Ultimately, morals are relative to the stage of a society's development. Both individual and collective actions are judged in terms of their promoting or hindering the achievement of Communism.

To the outside observer it appears that the Soviets operate on the assumption that the ends, being correct and supported by the course of history, validate the means and override such less relevant subjective matters as irrational morals and ethics. This often seems to be the Soviet ethical basis for international behavior although one does find moralizing and even moral indignation in their public statements about foreign affairs, such as those concerning Nazi Germany or Chinese border activities. It is probably more accurate to say that their basis for taking a moral position is utilitarian in that the rightness or wrongness of an action is judged first in relation to the circumstances of the society in question at that time and place, and then in terms of the consequences for achieving Communism which, as they see it, is the ultimate utopian condition of man and society.[15] As this pattern of thinking is expressed in the international behavior of the Soviet Union, their style in debate and negotiations and their policy decisions stand in contrast to that of most other nations.

The Communist mood in foreign affairs is understandably combative. The Communist conception of the historical process is one of unavoidable struggle among antagonistic forces, of "burying capitalism" in the long run. There is propriety and even virtue in using pressure and force—although not necessarily military force—to gain Communist objectives. The enemy is defined by the doctrine, so that aside from pursuing the national interest objectives traditionally recognized in international affairs, the Soviets find it in their self-interest, and in the interest of utopian socialism, to be belligerent toward "capitalism" and "imperialism." Peace short of the goal is seen more as a necessary tactic or stratagem than as a desirable state of affairs in itself.

Further, since the Soviets judge events and issues in the long view of process and historical evolution, time and the immediacy of international problems are necessarily viewed differently. The ethos is utopian; the strategy and objective are to move the process along, not necessarily to settle the issue or solve the problem at hand, unless such action is consistent with the long view. This reasoning conflicts sharply with the American penchant for direct action and for visible and immediate solutions. This does not mean that the Communist theory will never allow accommodation on an issue, or allow a retreat from a position. Such action, "rationally" taken, is proper when the situation demands, as in chess. But the long view, the process, and the ultimate objective theoretically are not lost.

The Soviet system, substantially reinforced by Russian society, presents a special outlook on the function of government itself. It should not be forgotten that the Communist governmental regime continues some basic features of long standing. A strong centralized state, headed by a partially deified ruler with unlimited authority, administered by a large bureaucracy, and controlled by a secret and political police using censorship and repression was the normal daily fare for many years of czarist government.

The system rests on a conception of the relationship between the individual and government which contrasts sharply with the American societal view. Even before the October Revolution, Russian culture tended to establish the individual's identity in the context of the group, whether in the *mir*, or peasant community, or in urban social organizations. In the *mir*, which was organized by household units, decisions were made in a council of elders with its chairman. Discussion might be considerable but the decision, announced by the leader rather than voted on, was asserted to be unanimous, or at least acquiesced in passively after everyone had been heard. There was a folk mystical belief in the sanctity and rightness of these decisions as embodying the will of the group; the individual who objected was out of line.

Except for a rising intellectual elite, the individual did not seek special enlightenment on his own or think in terms of personal rights or of self-reliant personal achievement. Traditionally, the individual was psychologically oriented toward affiliation and a sense of belonging within the emotional security of a group; he had group identity before personal identity. At the peasant base the individual was orthodox; he left collective problems to communal resolution, and those on a national scale to God and to the Czar. He did not see himself as an active agent trying to control his universe.[16]

We suggested earlier that Americans see government as a mechanism and as a method for reaching group decisions and for executing policies, with the people deciding the way in which the government should go. Americans tolerate the government's power as necessary to assure protection of personal liberty. The picture which one gets from studies of Soviet society is that the government is supposed to hold the expert knowledge and understanding of the collective problem.[17] Its function is to know the way to go, to control and coordinate, and to supply the direction and the restraint which the individual lacks. In this sense the Russian identifies with the power of the state, with the assumption that his own interests are bound up in it. Almost the reverse of the American expectation that government is the people's machinery, Soviet government and society are inseparable; the public interest and the government's interest, theoretically, are the same. The Byzantine legacy of government reinforced by the church provides a theological cast to this pattern of thinking.

When the system did not work, habitual reasoning would place the blame on bureaucratic wrongdoing or mismanagement, and relief would be sought from the head of the state. It was an extreme step to change the authority at the top; there was no precedent for calling new parliamentary elections.

Soviet government, then, is conceived not as a government of laws, but more as a government of men with special talent for knowing what is in the society's interest, or in Communist terms, men with special access to scientific truth and correct interpretation. It is not so much a government *by* the people as *for* the people. According to the evidence available, the individual is not very concerned with his inviolable rights as far as government is concerned, but he does expect the government to respect his dignity as a person—and this is not the same thing. He expects government to be predictable and consistent in exercising its authority. Studies of refugees seem to show that the Communist regime's omnipresent police control has not bothered Soviet citizens as much as its arbitrariness and capriciousness.[18]

Paternalistic government is expected. Escapees, for instance, did not criticize this presumption of government, in fact they assumed that the government should attend to the citizen's needs in education, medicine, old age assistance, etc., on a collective basis. Also, state ownership and control of the means of production, as a general concept, is not too inconsistent with traditional Russian thinking, at least when compared with contrasting American and related Western expectations. Even in czarist times the state played a prominent role in selecting and promoting private industry, both domestic and foreign, and in maintaining a close government-business relationship. The idea of the government-controlled collective farm, on the other hand, has encountered opposition in popular attitudes and outlooks, not so much for the general collective approach as for the way in which impersonal government bureaucracy has conflicted with sentimental bonds of community and friendship, and in many cases has deprived the peasant family of its private use of a plot of land. The psychological fallout from this state interference still seems to plague the "objective" and "scientific" program of the central government.

Earlier we referred to differing conceptions of democratic participation in government as focusing on either political or economic concerns. Soviet society has tended to be more preoccupied with economic than with political participation, which normally was left to political elites. Thus the objectives of a socialist state do not violate the Russian's conception of "democracy," although he may fuss about the details. Any strong value orientation supporting capitalism apparently was a minority view, and its demise was taken in fairly easy stride by most of the rural population and the labor force.

When all this is put together and extended to perceptions regarding international institutions such as the United Nations and its agencies, a patterned Soviet approach can be anticipated. While the Americans may expect these agencies to provide the forum and ground rules by which reasonable men can resolve problems, compromise, and cooperate on common objectives, the Communist view is that if these institutions are to accomplish anything worthwhile, they must operate within the "scientific" facts of life, where the theory should be objectively correct. As they see it, one cannot say that there is some truth on each side of an argument. If these international institutions do not fulfill this potential, then the Soviet conception of their function reverts to their general expectation in dealing with forces outside the Communist scheme of things, that is, to the level of tactics and stratagems which will promote the process toward socialism. There would, theoretically, be no basis for working for pragmatic compromises to resolve problems at hand unless there is a tactical advantage in doing so, for how can one compromise with the "truth" of science, or the "right" solution? In fact, "compromise" is not a traditionally valued way to reach decisions, and Lenin advised specifically against it for its own sake as not being worthy of the march of Communism. Therefore, the official Soviet representative approaches deliberations in the United Nations, for example, with perceptions which usually do not mesh with Western thought, and the Western negotiator must routinely depend on arguments which will convince the Soviet representation that it is tactically best to accommodate, perhaps to avoid catastrophe, or to avoid losing ground in their longer-range objectives. It may not be too much to say that Russian negotiators never really compromise, they maneuver or they adapt.

We would expect the underlying rationale for a Soviet style and manner in international affairs to be based partly on Communist ideology, and partly on background Russian modal personality factors. Diplomats feel that Russian leaders traditionally have been suspicious, intolerant, devious, and distrustful of diplomatic practice; unable to understand Western values and ideas, assume good will in motivation, or see a peace treaty as more than a provisional armistice subservient to a Russian messianic role in history.[19] However, because leadership and government responsibility are more confined to a mentally-disciplined elite in the current Soviet system, the balance in diplomatic approach may shift more to the formal logic side of the Communist system as far as reactions, perceptions, and reasoning are concerned. This shift is especially evident when compared to other approaches in which theory is expected to play a less explicit role, as in United States policy reasoning, where the logic of everyday affairs will tend to apply across the board.

The basic assumption that the interpretation of truth and knowledge of the right course of history are the privileged possession of the Soviet government and the system's demand for disciplined adherence to that interpretation seems to explain the official Soviet style in routine negotiation and debate. Certainly it helps explain the frequent need to seek instructions. Logically, public opinion or the approval of those assembled in debate are considered less important, and are taken into account more for selection of tactic than for influencing decisions regarding the objective itself. Basically they assume the role of negotiator in behalf of the socialist movement in general, and for a constituency which goes far beyond the U.S.S.R. itself. In debate there appears to be less reason to discuss issues in detail or to see serious purpose in exchanging views, for there is an implied fruitlessness in such endeavor. How can one discuss when one side is completely correct and the other completely wrong? Hence the Soviet officials' style in debate is one of "correctly" defining the issue and the principles involved, from which they see results following automatically. There is a tendency to be unimpressed with new facts, and to perceive such facts in a way that is consistent with the theory and the "right" solution. So the facts are bent to fit the theory. This practice is frequently reported from the U.S.S.R. when production statistics are provided, for example. The report must fit the plan whatever mental gymnastics or behind-the-scenes manipulation are required. There is a certain willingness to live in a fiction rather than challenge the policy which, by definition, is correct. At worst, the facts may require a reinterpretation of the theory.

Although Soviet leaders enjoy a great deal of privacy in making foreign policy, their decisions too are influenced by the public diplomacy factor. What would the Russian approach and style be if there were no Communist regime? Russia has a long history of either direct participation in, or immediate concern with, European power politics and the often bitter contests for power and survival which have dominated European international relations for many generations. This involvement leaves a stamp of preoccupations and perceptions regarding relations with neighboring territories which are basically Russian, not necessarily Communist. Despite their own ethnic diversity, the Russians have long held a sense of nationalism and a concern for the greatness and manifest destiny of Russia, which did not start with the Communists in 1917.

The fact that throughout history Russia has been predominantly a rural society, much more so than her neighbors to the west, has a certain psychological pertinence. Russians have been conscious of their less than prestigious image in more industrialized and refined centers of Europe. They often were considered gross and uncultured country bumpkins; only the educated Russian elites were considered the exceptions. Hence today there is a special and persistent Russian interest in promoting national artistic, educational, and scientific excellence, and an assumption that it is the government's role to foster it. Travelers report a widespread and genuine Russian pride in accomplishment, and desire that it be recognized. The rapid progress which the Soviet Union has enjoyed, despite the high cost (as seen by outsiders), is a source of both national pride and national ethos which is pertinent to the present-day national character. It seems to have produced something of a work ethic and a Russian-style achievement motivation; collective participation in conquering their "frontier" may have produced an imprint on the Russian outlook which corresponds to that produced many years earlier in the United States.[20] All this contributes to a pattern of Russian assumptions about themselves and the world which is part of their cognitive basis for governmental programs and policies.

Other cognitive factors could be examined at the public level; for example, various elements in the Russian psychological world have produced a distinctive perception of "aggression." The memory of war on Russian soil remains vivid. Issues such as rectifying borders or defending against invasion are public anxieties. This theme is found repeatedly in Russian novels, theater, and art. According to the social psychologist Ralph White, the Russians see themselves as the area's most peace-loving people, with the greatest reason to be so, and they tend to perceive foreign actions such as the American U-2 flights as more threatening and more emotionally and dramatically posed than the foreign power might anticipate. Although this belief in their own peaceful intent does not appear consistent with the Communist theory of struggle and violence, it does seem to be the popular view, and gives rise to public nervousness regarding potential conflict on Russia's borders.[21]

Conclusion :

Reasonable Expectations

for Applying New Concepts

THE TEST OF ALL THAT HAS BEEN SAID IS, OF COURSE, whether it contributes to a better understanding of communications problems in international affairs, and especially to anticipating the patterns of perception and response which can make a big difference in how a foreign policy proposal will actually work out. We assume that the psychological dimension will become more significant, not less, as time goes on. Communication technology is expanding its capabilities and its effects. Public participation in international affairs processes will certainly increase.

For these reasons the competent professional in foreign affairs will be harder pressed to deal with what might be called the "cognitive milieu" in his sphere of policy interest. This means that still more competence will be needed at all levels of policy machinery in working with the philosophical premises, value orientations, and conceptions of law and international affairs held by foreign policy makers. It also means—and this is the additional dimension—more competence in comprehending the public psychological factors treated in the preceding pages.

One must, for analytical purposes, find a way to place oneself

outside the communication process itself, to rise above identification with any of the participants in order to establish objectively both the actual *facts* of the situation and the *psychology*
of the communication situation. Said another way, the observer
must try to establish both the objective reality of an international
issue and the "reality" as perceived by the parties to the communication or negotiation, including the "reality" perceived by
the observer's own side. The view from such a position can be
startling.

Several behavioral scientists and international relations specialists have tried to achieve this view in an attempt to untangle
the elements which affect international interaction processes. A
whole issue of the *Journal of International Affairs* was devoted
to the subject "Image and Reality in World Politics," [1] with attention directed toward such international confrontations as the
cold war, China and the West, the Viet Nam conflict, and the
First World War. Ralph White's book *Nobody Wanted War*,[2]
a social-psychological approach, is a striking suggestion that all
sides involved in Viet Nam held serious misperceptions of the
motivations and intentions of the other parties. Harrison E. Salisbury discusses the psychological "reality" of various sides in his
article "Image and Reality in Indochina," [3] and Joseph H. de
Rivera tries to reconstruct the individual perceptions which led
to decisions taken in the Korean War in *The Psychological Dimension of Foreign Policy*.[4] The purpose in publishing the perio-
dical *Journal of Conflict Resolution* is in part to study conflicting perception and other basic factors in aggression and conflict.
A team of social psychologists in Great Britain actually assembled
groups of officials from countries involved in standing conflicts
such as the Cyprus problem to undertake laboratory negotiation
sessions which would allow them to study the conflicting perceptions reflected in the exchange.[5]

Gaming and simulation have been used, with varying degrees
of success and applicability, to direct attention to this dimension
of international negotiation and interaction. The difficulty in

these exercises is that when the participants are all from the same culture, contrasting perceptions injected into the simulation are artificial at best, and often the most significant perceptions escape attention altogether.

Perhaps in some cases the various attempts to probe the psychological dimension have concentrated too much on the national policy level of perception, and have involved speculation beyond the support available in complete and hard data. Still, the findings concerning the international conflict situations they examine are much more useful than those that have evolved from analyses which rest only on conventional wisdom or which view the situation through the eyes of one party to the conflict. Certainly the same above-the-action perspective is useful in many situations more limited in scope, communication, and interaction, as, for example, when using role analysis. However, whatever the level of analysis chosen, surely this kind of approach points the direction for the diplomacy of the future.

We recognize that international communication involves much more than the psychological base. We also need to understand the structure of communications processes in a given time and place to judge how psychological factors might bear on a foreign policy issue. This facet of the problem has received only passing mention here, but this does not imply that it should receive second priority attention. Nations can be studied as communications systems. Governments gear into these systems in differing ways, the more so as the varying forms of new national governments enter the scene. The communications role of politically conscious elites differs widely from one country to the next. Communications technology differs, and is controlled in diverse ways. Groups and institutions interact in distinct patterns. It is a long path from underlying perception habits to actual consequences in a government's foreign policy.

The problem is, to paraphrase an old cliché, that culture and psychology in foreign affairs are too important to be left to the behavioral scientists. We must use them more, and we must encourage their research in foreign affairs problems. But practically we know that we will not be using specialists from the behavioral science field at all the important points where their insight is needed. Even if we tried, they would need to know much more about foreign affairs than they do to be helpful on short notice.

Some substantial degree of competence in handling cultural and psychological factors needs to be part of the equipment of everyone concerned with foreign affairs, particularly the professionals. They need to have enough understanding of the nature of these factors to know what they are looking for, to know what the questions are. They need to know how behavioral science approaches to foreign affairs problems have been made in other times and places. They need conceptual and observational tools to help organize and analyze the information available around them.

Even with the best academic training in most of today's international studies programs, one leaves the protected classroom unprepared to find out how much psychological imponderables are mixed into the real life of international affairs. While the emphasis on perception presented here may not turn out to be the optimum integrating concept, eventually the cultural and psychological dimension will receive greater attention, and will compete in the curricula with traditional offerings in diplomatic history and international law and politics. Better exposure to behavioral science concepts will add a necessary facet to intellectual preparation for the foreign affairs field, and should not be delayed.

Extensive effort has been expended in international studies circles during the last few years to develop theory in international relations. A substantial part of this effort has been directed at a macro or global level of analysis by which theorists seek to establish the regularities in the way that nations, as units, interact in an international system in correlation with measurable variables —perhaps kind of government, size, military strength, degree of industrialization or any of a wide range of factors which could be proposed as relevant. The availability of computer technology has encouraged these efforts to be scientific in studying the behavior of nations, and to stretch the term "behavioral approach" to apply to these methods. So far the scientific validity of their models, premises, means of defining and measuring, and size of samples leaves much to be desired. At times they have chosen to study problems because they lend themselves to method rather than because they are particularly significant. In any case, the global level of the interrelationships under study promises little immediate practical utility for the diplomat or decision maker. Whether the products of this research will aid the long-range planner remains to be seen.[6]

For the much less global level of perception and reasoning treated in these chapters, there is also some question as to how scientifically one can proceed. But at least there has been substantial progress in meeting some of the criteria for scientific methodology and analysis. The conceptual tools of the behavioral sciences have proven themselves capable of defining and isolating many of the important factors in human behavior, and in some cases doing so with enough precision to allow testing and measuring. They have withstood the test of reducing what appears to be random or intuitively described behavior to patterns which allow an appreciable degree of prediction. The traditional behavioral science disciplines had to back away from the global theories of a Spengler or a Toynbee to concentrate on a more manageable middle range combination of theory and investigation. This precedent suggests that such a more limited objective would be fruitful in the international relations field. For this endeavor the behavioral sciences offer a lead. There is much yet to be done to establish these disciplines as mature sciences, but they have considerable practical utility now even for those who only want to use them to sharpen their intellectual equipment for the era of public diplomacy unfolding before us.

Notes

I. The Relevance of the Behavioral Sciences to Modern Diplomacy

1. Harold Nicolson, *Diplomacy* (London: Oxford University Press, 2d ed., 1950).

2. This demand on the capacities of foreign service personnel is recognized in the Department of State's current projection for management and organizational reform. See *Diplomacy for the 70's: A Program of Management Reform for the Department of State*, Department of State Publication #8551 (Washington, D.C.: U.S. Government Printing Office, December 1970), p. 112.

3. This subject commands a large literature, of course. See, for example, W. Phillips Davison, *International Political Communication* (New York: Praeger, 1965).

4. In recent years a number of university programs have added emphasis to some aspect of international communication, with international journalism often a salient aspect. See, for example, the report on a 1969 symposium: James W. Markham (ed.), *International Communication as a Field of Study* (Iowa City: International Communications Division, Association for Education in Journailsm, 1970), distributed by Publications Department, University of Iowa.

5. U.S., Congress, House, Committee on Foreign Affairs, *The Future of United States Public Diplomacy* (Report No. 6 by the Subcommittee on International Organizations and Movements, H.R. 179, 90th Cong., 2d sess., 1968). A summary is available in the Department of State News Letter, #93, January 1969.

6. U.S., Congress, Senate, Committee on Foreign Relations, *Psychological Aspects of Foreign Policy* (Hearings on June 5, 19, and 20, 1969. 91st Cong., 1st sess.).

7. Heinz Eulau, *The Behavioral Persuasion in Politics* (New York: Random House, 1963).

8. From the editor's introductory chapter, Marian D. Irish (ed.), *Political Science: Advance of the Discipline* (Englewood Cliffs, N.J.: Prentice-Hall, 1968), p. 10.

9. W. Phillips Davison has made a comprehensive review of the use of American behavioral scientists in foreign affairs deliberations in his article "Foreign Policy," in Paul F. Lazarsfeld, William H. Sewell, and Harold L. Wilensky (eds.), *The Uses of Sociology* (New York: Basic Books, 1967).

10. Oscar Lewis, *The Children of Sanchez* (New York: Random House, 1961).

11. Ruth Benedict, *The Chrysanthemum and the Sword: Patterns of Japanese Culture* (Boston: Houghton Mifflin, 1946).

12. Margaret Mead, *And Keep Your Powder Dry: An Anthropologist Looks at America* (New York: William Morrow, 1942).

13. Several summaries of the culture and personality field are available. For a brief item, see Adamson E. Hoebel, "Anthropological Perspectives on National Character," *Annals of the American Academy of Political and Social Science*, vol. 370 (March 1967). Or see longer treatments in Bert Kaplan (ed.), *Studying Personality Cross-Culturally* (Evanston, Ill.: Row, Peterson, 1961), or Alex Inkeles and Daniel J. Levinson, "National Character: The Study of Modal Personality and Sociocultural Systems," in Gardner Lindzey (ed.), *The Handbook of Social Psychology*, vol. IV (Menlo Park, Cal.: Addison-Wesley Publishing Co., 2d ed., 1969).

14. Two of the early examples in this field are Otto Klineberg, *Tensions Affecting International Understanding: A Survey of Research* (New York: Social Science Research Council, 1950); and William Buchanan and Hadley Cantril, *How Nations See Each Other* (Urbana: University of Illinois Press, 1953). A more recent review of the field is provided in Herbert C. Kelman (ed.), *International Behavior: A Social-Psychological Analysis* (New York: Holt, Rinehart and Winston, 1965).

15. An article by Stanley Hoffman further encourages one to use a perception analysis. He demonstrates how the basic approach adopted in relations between states is affected by contrasting perceptions of the issues, the procedure of negotiation, and the world view of the states themselves. See his "Perceptions, Reality, and the Franco-American Conflict," *International Affairs*, vol. XXI, no. 1 (1967).

II. Perceiving the Issues: A Study in Comparative Psychology

1. For a discussion of the role of the Emperor during this critical period, see Kazuo Kawai, *Japan's American Interlude* (Chicago: University of Chicago Press, 1960), especially Chapter V. For an account of the study project from the American side, see Alexander H. Leighton and Morris Edward Opler, "Psychiatry and Applied Anthropology in Psychological Warfare Against Japan," *American Journal of Psychoanalysis*, vol. 6 (1946); reprinted in Wilbur Schramm (ed.), *The Process and Effects of Mass Communication* (Urbana: University of Illinois Press, 1961), pp. 157–69.

2. For a more concentrated treatment see Franklin P. Kilpatrick (ed.), *Explorations in Transactional Psychology* (New York: New York University Press, 1961). "Transaction" is the term for an analytical convenience by which one slices out a segment in time and space to examine the functional relationships between environment and perception as parts of an indissoluble whole.

3. There is some confusion in the literature because the term "reality world" has sometimes been used to mean the individual's conception of his own world, or what I have called "psychological world." It seems preferable to avoid reverse meanings, however.

4. A somewhat dated but still relevant discussion of perceiving the world is Chapter III in David Krech and Richard S. Crutchfield, *Theory and Problems of Social Psychology* (New York: McGraw-Hill, 1948).

5. See Leon Festinger, *The Theory of Cognitive Dissonance* (Evanston, Ill.: Row, Peterson, 1957). This conceptual approach has been used by a large group of psychologists, and is now part of the basic vocabulary in social psychology.

6. I am indebted to Dr. John Gillin for this approach, as well as for many other general conceptualizations in the culture and personality field which lend themselves so directly to public diplomacy analysis. He was my friend and teacher, and the author of *The Ways of Men* (New York: Appleton-Century, 1948), a text which has inspired many anthropology students to pursue their discipline in the context of the broader behavioral science field.

7. For a short summary of the subject by a recognized authority, see Otto Klineberg, "Racial Psychology," in Ralph Linton (ed.), *The Science of Man in the World Crisis* (New York: Columbia University Press, 1945), pp. 63–77.

8. David Riesman, *The Lonely Crowd* (New Haven: Yale University Press, abridged ed., 1961).

9. William H. Whyte, *The Organization Man* (New York: Simon and Schuster, 1956).

10. See John Gillin, "Some Signposts for Policy," in Richard Adams (ed.), *Social Change in Latin America Today* (New York: Vintage Books, 1960). For a still more direct summary of a Latin American psychological world, see "If I Were a Brazilian," in Charles Wagley, *An Introduction to Brazil* (New York: Columbia University Press, 1963), Chapter 7.

11. This confusion in meaning is one of the problems in Washington Platt's *National Character in Action: Intelligence Factors in Foreign Relations* (New Brunswick, N.J.: Rutgers University Press, 1961). Platt tends to see national character as the "character" of the nation.

12. Two good summaries on this subject are available: Alex Inkeles and Daniel J. Levinson, "National Character: The Study of Modal Personality and Sociocultural Systems," in Gardner Lindzey (ed.), *The Handbook of Social Psychology*, vol. IV (Menlo Park, Cal.: Addison-Wesley Publishing Co. 2d ed., 1969); and Milton Singer, "A Survey of Culture and Personality Theory and Research," in Bert Kaplan (ed.), *Studying Personality Cross-Culturally* (Evanston, Ill.: Row, Peterson, 1961).

13. Two books by Edward T. Hall explore this general subject: *The Silent Language* (Garden City, N.Y.: Doubleday, 1959); and *The Hidden Dimension* (Garden City, N.Y.: Doubleday, 1966).

14. David D. McClelland, *The Achieving Society* (Princeton: Van Nostrand, 1961).

15. David D. McClelland and David G. Winter, *Motivating Economic Achievement* (New York: The Free Press, 1969).

III. Differing Points of View below the National Surface

1. These terms are found, for example, in G. A. Almond and J. S. Coleman (eds.), *The Politics of the Developing Areas* (Princeton: Princeton University Press, 1960), which contributed some important new ideas to the field.

2. For a summary of current political science approaches in developing areas, see David Apter and Charles Andrain, "Comparative Government: Developing New Nations," in Marian D. Irish (ed.), *Political Science* (Englewood Cliffs, N.J.: Prentice-Hall, 1968).

3. An outstanding example is Lucien W. Pye (ed.), *Communica-*

tions and Political Development (Princeton: Princeton University Press, 1963).

4. This aspect of international interaction is consistent with the current interest in political science in "linkage politics." This interest is a recognition that while for purposes of analysis a delimited political system, a nation, for example, is arbitrarily chosen, some interest groups of that system are linked with counterpart groups in other systems, and it is shown that their political behavior is affected accordingly. See James N. Rosenau (ed.), *Linkage Politics: Essays on the Convergence of National and International Systems* (New York: The Free Press, 1969).

5. Carlton Coon, *Caravan: The Story of the Middle East* (New York: Henry Holt, 1951).

6. W. Lloyd Warner and Paul S. Lunt, *The Social Life of a Modern Community* (New Haven: Yale University Press, 1941).

7. David Lerner, *The Passing of Traditional Society* (Glencoe, Ill., The Free Press, 1958).

8. Considerable political science attention is being paid to new elites. For examples see Frederick W. Frey, *The Turkish Political Elite* (Cambridge: M.I.T. Press, 1965); or John J. Johnson, *The Military and Society in Latin America* (Stanford: Stanford University Press, 1964).

9. Winston S. Churchill, *The Second World War* (abridged one-volume edition, Boston: Houghton Mifflin, 1948). My attention was first called to this striking example of changing role behavior by a dramatized educational radio series, "Ways of Mankind," directed in the 1950s by Walter Goldschmidt.

10. James N. Mosel, a social psychologist, has studied and written on the subject of role behavior in Thailand. Using experience there as case-study material, he has lectured at the Foreign Service Institute of the Department of State for a number of years. As a result role analysis is one of the behavioral science concepts to which an appreciable percentage of U.S. government overseas personnel have been exposed.

11. A particularly well-organized study of bureaucracy under change is that of the Indian Administrative service carried out by Richard P. Taub. See his *Bureaucrats Under Stress: Administrators and Administration in an Indian State* (Berkeley: University of California Press, 1969). Another well-known source is Joseph Lapalombara (ed.), *Bureaucracy and Political Development* (Princeton: Princeton University Press, 1963).

IV. How Preconceptions about Institutions Affect
International Communication

1. Walter Lippmann, *Public Opinion* (New York: Harcourt, Brace and Co., 1922). Also in paperback (New York: The Free Press, 1965).

2. Robert K. Merton, *Social Theory and Social Structure* (Glencoe, Ill.: The Free Press, 1949). A number of sociologists have contributed to structure-function theory, but the terminology which Merton used to crystalize the concept was the first to win wide acceptance.

3. Talcott Parsons' work spans several volumes, most of them difficult for the layman as well as for many social scientists. A key work was *The Social System* (Glencoe, Ill.: The Free Press, 1951). *Toward a General Theory of Action* (with E. Shils) has been a more specific source (Cambridge: Harvard University Press, 1951). For a more readable summary and critique of Parsons' work, see Max Black (ed.), *The Social Theories of Talcott Parsons* (Englewood Cliffs, N.J.: Prentice-Hall, 1961). Not all students of comparative politics feel that the Parsons contribution is a breakthrough in political theory. For example, see Joseph Lapalombara, "Parsimony and Empiricism in Comparative Politics," in Robert T. Holt and John E. Turner (eds.), *The Methodology of Comparative Research* (New York: The Free Press, 1970).

4. Heinz Eulau, for example, reviews this development in *The Behavioral Persuasion in Politics* (New York: Random House, 1963).

5. The subject of transplanting democratic institutions into the developing political systems of the new states, and the whole question of the function of government in such societies has elicited considerable political science attention. A number of stimulating approaches have been made. Two frequently mentioned items are: Gabriel A. Almond and Sidney Verba, *The Civic Culture: Political Attitudes and Democracy in Five Nations* (Boston: Little, Brown, 1965); and Samuel Huntington, *Political Order in Changing Societies* (New Haven: Yale University Press, 1968).

6. William Cameron Forbes, *The Philippine Islands*, 2 vols. (New York: Houghton Mifflin, 1928), vol. I, p. 141. This work is something of a classic account of the early period of U.S. administration of the Philippines.

V. Language, Perception, and Reasoning

1. S. I. Hayakawa, *Language in Thought and Action* (New York: Harcourt, Brace and World, 2d ed., 1964).

2. Stuart Chase, *Power of Words* (New York: Harcourt, Brace and Co., 1953).

3. Ibid., pp. 4–5.

4. In general, this progression in patterns of logic is the explanation made by Stuart Chase in *Power of Words* and in his foreword to the collection of Whorf's writings cited in note 5.

5. Benjamin Lee Whorf, *Language, Thought, and Reality* (Cambridge: M.I.T. Press, 1964, in paperback; first published by M. I. T. Press in 1956). For Edward Sapir's writings, see David G. Mandelbaum (ed.), *Culture, Language, and Personality* (Berkeley: University of California Press, condensed version, 1964).

6. Whorf, p. 214; also cited in Chase, p. 104.

7. For a technical review of some of the work done by psychologists in studying the relationships among language, perception, and behavior, see Roger Brown, *Words and Things* (New York: The Free Press, 1958); or George A. Miller and David McNeill, "Psycholinguistics," in Gardner Lindzey (ed.), *The Handbook of Social Psychology*, vol. III (Menlo Park, Cal.: Addison-Wesley Publishing Co., 2d ed., 1969).

8. April 8, 1967.

9. Lorand B. Szalay, Won T. Moon, and Jean Bryson, *Communication Lexicon on Three South Korean Audiences* (Washington, D.C.: American Institutes for Research, 1971).

10. Salvador de Madariaga, *Englishmen, Frenchmen, Spaniards: An Essay in Comparative Psychology* (London: Oxford University Press, 1928).

11. R.A.D. Forrest, *The Chinese Language* (London: Faber and Faber, 2d ed., 1965) might be more understandable to readers accustomed to a more traditional treatment of language than that found in the modern linguistic science school.

12. Dell Hymes discusses pitfalls in carrying the implications of differences in language content too far in making comparative studies of political systems. See "Linguistic Aspects of Comparative Political Research," in Robert T. Holt and John E. Turner (eds.), *The Methodology of Comparative Research* (New York: The Free Press, 1970).

13. For example, see Ralph White, "Socialism and Capitalism: An International Misunderstanding," *Foreign Affairs* (January 1966).

14. Edmund S. Glenn, "Meaning and Behavior: Communication and Culture," *The Journal of Communication*, vol. XVI, no. 4 (December 1966).

15. This example was suggested by the dramatized radio series on anthropological subjects, "Ways of Mankind," directed by Walter Goldschmidt, of the University of California, Los Angeles. The scripts have been published in Walter Goldschmidt (ed.), *Ways of Mankind* (Boston: The Beacon Press, 1954).

16. For example, in the Department of State, Edmund Glenn, as Chief of the Interpreters Branch, conducted seminars for interpreter personnel in which the metalinguistic dilemmas found in official translating and interpreting were discussed and explored.

17. Chase, p. 106.

18. For further discussion see Brown, Chapter VIII.

19. The summary presented here is somewhat interpretive. See Bryant Wedge, "Communication Analysis and Comprehensive Diplomacy," in Arthur S. Hoffman (ed.), *International Communication and the New Diplomacy* (Bloomington: Indiana University Press, 1968).

20. Glenn, op. cit.

21. Bilingualism presents a number of areas for further study where social and political processes are concerned. Problems of inner conflict arise within bilingual individuals as differing, and often conflicting, self-images, group and political identifications, and definitions of the situation need to be accommodated as these the individuals have occasion to switch languages. This was the subject of one issue of the *Journal of Social Issues*, "Problems of Bilingualism," edited by John Macnamara, vol. XXIII, no. 2 (April 1967).

22. *Manila Chronicle*, October 20, 1961.

VI. From Patterns of Thinking to the Behavior of Nations

1. Joseph H. de Rivera, *The Psychological Dimension of Foreign Policy* (Columbus, Ohio: Charles E. Merrill, 1968).

2. See George F. Kennan, *American Diplomacy: 1900–1950* (Chicago: University of Chicago Press, 1951; also Mentor Books, paperback).

3. This thesis is found in various places in Morgenthau's writings during that period. For a concise statement, see his "The Mainsprings of American Foreign Policy," *American Political Science Review* (December 1950).

4. For one key discussion of the problem, see Graham T. Allison, "Conceptual Models and the Cuban Missile Crisis," *American Political Science Review,* vol. LXIII, no. 3 (September 1969).

5. Frank Tannenbaum, *The American Tradition in Foreign Policy* (Norman: University of Oklahoma Press, 1955).

6. See Robert A. Lystad, "Cultural and Psychological Factors," in Vernon McKay (ed.), *African Diplomacy: Studies in the Determination of Foreign Policy* (New York: Praeger, 1966).

7. Edmund S. Glenn, "The Two Faces of Nationalism," *Comparative Political Studies* (October 1970).

8. Stanley Hoffmann, "Perceptions, Reality, and the Franco-American Conflict," *Journal of International Affairs,* vol. XXI, no. 1 (1967).

9. For example, Chapters VI and XIV in K. J. Holsti, *International Politics: A Framework for Analysis* (Englewood Cliffs, N.J.: Prentice-Hall, 1967).

10. Frederick H. Hartmann, *The New Age of American Foreign Policy* (New York: Macmillan, 1970).

11. Stephen H. Rhinesmith, "Cross-Cultural Communication in International Negotiation: A Case Study of the Drafting of the Universal Declaration of Human Rights" (Unpublished master's thesis, University of Pittsburgh Graduate School of Public and International Affairs, 1966).

12. For light reading on this period, see Hope Ridings Miller, *Embassy Row: The Life and Times of Diplomatic Washington* (New York: Holt, Rinehart and Winston, 1969).

13. Literature on the subject is vast; for one concise and readily available summary, see Bertram D. Wolfe, "Communist Ideology and Soviet Foreign Policy," *Foreign Affairs,* vol. 41, no. 1 (October 1962).

14. Again the literature is large. A well-known item is Zbigniew K. Brzezinski, *Ideology and Power in Soviet Politics* (New York: Praeger, rev. ed., 1967).

15. For a comprehensive discussion of the moralistic orientation, see Richard T. DeGeorge, *Soviet Ethics and Morality* (Ann Arbor: University of Michigan Press, 1969).

16. Compared with the literature on Soviet politics and ideology, little is available in the behavioral sciences on cultural and psychological factors related to Soviet government. A convenient summary based on the Human Relations Area Files is Thomas Fitzsimmons, Peter Malof, and John C. Fiske, *USSR* (New Haven: HRAF Press, 1960). Two other sources are often cited: Raymond A. Bauer, Alex Inkeles, and Clyde Kluckhohn, *How the Soviet System Works* (Cam-

bridge: Harvard University Press, 1956), one of several publications resulting from a Harvard Research Team study of the Soviet Union, with data taken largely from defectors and refugees; and Margaret Mead, *Soviet Attitudes Toward Authority* (New York: William Morrow, 1955), also a report of a team research project.

17. A further reference on the contrasting American and Soviet view of government, and one used here is Anatol Rapoport, "Perceiving the Cold War," in Roger Fisher (ed.), *International Conflict and Behavioral Science* (New York: Basic Books, 1964).

18. This kind of material is found in another publication of the Harvard Research Team: Alex Inkeles and Raymond A. Bauer, *The Soviet Citizen: Daily Life in a Totalitarian Society* (Cambridge: Harvard University Press, 1959). See also Alex Inkeles, Eugenia Hanfmann, and Helen Beier, "Modal Personality and Adjustment to the Soviet Socio-Political System," in Bert Kaplan (ed.), *Studying Personality Cross-Culturally* (New York: Harper and Row, 1961).

19. Fitzsimmons, Malof, and Fiske, op. cit.

20. This outlook appears in various selections in Paul Hollander's edited collection of articles on comparative sociology, *American and Soviet Society* (Englewood Cliffs, N.J.: Prentice-Hall, 1969).

21. Ralph K. White, "Images in the Context of International Conflict: Soviet Perceptions of the U.S. and the U.S.S.R.," in Herbert C. Kelman (ed.), *International Behavior* (New York: Holt, Rinehart and Winston, 1965).

Conclusion: Reasonable Expectations for Applying New Concepts

1. Vol. XXI, no. 1 (1967).

2. Ralph White, *Nobody Wanted War* (Garden City, N.Y.: Doubleday, 1968).

3. Harrison E. Salisbury, "Image and Reality in Indochina," *Foreign Affairs*, April 1971.

4. Joseph H. de Rivera, *The Psychological Dimension of Foreign Policy* (Columbus, Ohio: Charles E. Merrill, 1968).

5. Methodological problems, but not the substance of the debate, are discussed in John W. Burton, *Conflict and Communication: The Use of Controlled Communication in International Relations* (New York: The Free Press, 1969).

6. A summary of the state of affairs in international relations theory is available in Harry Howe Ransom's article "International Relations," in Marian D. Irish (ed.), *Political Science: Advance of the Discipline* (Englewood Cliffs, N.J.: Prentice-Hall, 1968).

Index

achievement: in American culture, 34, 40-42, 57, 58, 148; achievement motif, 34, 40-42, 57, 58, 148; optimism, 34, 144-45; materialism, 41-42, 59, 148; individualism, 57, 140; sin-guilt motif, 115-17, 148
Alger, Horatio, 33
Alliance for Progress, 8, 145
American Institute for Free Labor, 47
American culture: middle class in, 33, 57, 64, 148; achievement motif, 34, 40-42, 57, 58, 148; optimism, 34, 144-45; materialism, 41-42, 59, 148; individualism, 57, 140; sin-guilt motif, 115-17, 148
anthropology, cultural: contributions to international relations, 11, 13, 14-16
Arab conflict with Israel, 5, 51, 134
Aristotelian theory of language, 97-98

Barrientos, René, 125
Bay of Pigs incident, 9
"Beetle Bailey" comic strip, 56
Benedict, Ruth, 14, 16
bilingualism, 105-106, 174n.21

capitalism: "people's", 59; varying connotations of, 110
caste: defined, 57
Catholic Church: and international labor, 47
Chase, Stuart, 95, 98, 120
China, Communist: foreign policy, 136, 153
Chinese language, 100, 103-104, 115, 120
Churchill, Winston, 66

cognition, 23-25
cognitive dissonance: defined, 29
colonial administration: aided by anthropology, 14-15
color: words and the perception of, 99; comparison of synonyms for, 100
communication: and social role, 67-74
communism: and labor, 47, 48; compared with democratic ideology, 57-58; U.S. fear of, 149, spread of, by Soviets, 151, 152, 157-58
Coon, Carleton, 51
"co-ordinate state": explained, 132-33, 151
Coughlin, W. J., 95
Cousins, Norman, 100
cultural diffusion: and language adjustment, 108
cultural exchange programs, 29
culture and language, 96, 101-103, 105, 106
culture and personality: 16, 36-38, 80; studies, 16, 30
culture concept, 11, 15-16

Darlan, J. E., adm., 66
democracy: different concepts of, 141-42; Russian view, 156
Devlin, Bernadette, 51
diplomacy, public: defined, 7-8
diplomats: objectivity of, 5, 13, 128-29, 148, 162
Dulles, John F., 148

Ugly American, by William J. Lederer and Eugene Burdick, 128
UNESCO, 18
United Nations: becoming institutionalized, 81-82; languages used in, 109, 123; U.S. attitude toward, 138; debate on human rights, 140-41; Soviet concept of, 157
United States: space program, 7; materialism in, 41-42, 59, 148; achievement motif in, 40-42, 57, 58, 148; labor, 47-49; impact of Viet Nam war, 53-55; individualism in, 57, 140; administration of Philippines, 87-93, 133; attitude toward U.N., 138; ethnocentrism, 142, 143-44, 145; fear of communism, 149
U.S. House Foreign Affairs Committee, 8

U.S. Information Service, 6
U.S. Senate Committee on Foreign Relations, 8

Viet Nam, 52, 53-55

Warner, W. Lloyd, 56
Wedge, Bryant, 122-23
West Germany, 47
White, Ralph, 160, 162
White, William H., 33
Whorf, Benjamin L., 98-99, 114
Wilder, Thornton, 113
Wilson, Woodrow, 3, 148
words, new, 108

Yankee City studies, 56